A
SLOW
LEARNER
REMEMBERS

RALPH ROBINSON

ISBN: 9798671517132

COVER: Eleanor Jane Robinson, BA (hons)

ALSO BY RALPH ROBINSON

Abandon the Cave: Faith's Seductive Virtual Reality, Strategic
Book Publishing and Rights Co., Houston, Texas, 2012.
Leave Heaven to Angels and Sparrows, 2020.
Fables of Faith: Myth, Tradition and Scripture, 2020.
Good? Is God? Faith No More, 2020.
Think About It, 2020.

DEDICATION

The book is tribute to

Dr Shirley Schulz-Robinson who leads life fully, ever aware of how others are faring. She has eased life for many, her long career has always included concern for others: as an accomplished nurse alert to public health, a university educator, an advocate for people suffering mental distress, and her skills as a hypnotist and coach. I am grateful for her care and support.

Whilst this planet has gone circling
on according to the
fixed laws of gravity,
from so simple a beginning
endless forms most beautiful
and most wonderful have been and
are evolving.

Charles Darwin

closing *The Origin of Species*

CONTENTS

PREFACE

Orson Welles wrote a famous novel in 1898, *War of the Worlds*, imagining an invasion of earth by Martians. The BBC made a film series version of Welles' vivid book. The broadcast in October 1938 was preceded by an announcement which clearly stated that it was a theatrical programme. It was not universally admired by critics.

The reception by listeners was unexpected but notable. Many, who may had tuned in without hearing the preamble to the programme, took it as a news broadcast of an invasion by Martian aliens[1]. The unimaginable destruction and fearsome force envisaged excited terror. The resulting panic and confusion were reported to be extreme – some press claims were that millions of listeners reacted in wild panic. A fictional broadcast had resulted in vast numbers of people believing that so remarkable an invasion was *actual* and held immediate extreme danger for earth people.

There is a moral to this tale.

The broadcast was fictional. It "reported" calamitous events realistically enough to induce fearful panic in vast numbers of listeners. The fantasy was believed by many people and alarm was extreme. But the broadcast was spectacular vivid showmanship, no more.

The mass panic caused by the broadcast was not only fuelled by fiction. Welles wrote the novel when there was live speculation about extra-terrestrial life on Mars, advanced civilisations, and possibly hostile

---

[1] I have also read denial that wide panic ensued. Articles in the press were said to exaggerate the effect of the broadcast. For this essay, we will assume the press story was factually based as reported.

incursions of alien space dwellers. A broadcast complete with believable sound effects could readily be assumed as confirmation that these speculations had truly predicted so dire an event.

There was *no* actual basis for any fear or confusion. The World was not invaded. But belief in unexpected apocalypse was the more readily fearfully believed because of prior beliefs entertaining the possibility[2].

Belief, in this case, was far from knowledge.

The example is striking, yet relevant. In essays following in this book I have claimed that not all belief is sound. There are significant still popular folk beliefs which are held by individuals and affecting their decisions and actions.

Amongst these beliefs are some treasured by many, and thought indeed to be not only unquestionably true, but so compelling that life's gravest decisions rest on them. Such decisions are often made as if normal in one's family or ethnicity. Values and attitudes are taken for granted and lead to the customs and behaviours usual in the familiarity of one's environment. But so many, so different, and so many environments have valued traditions and myths. Humanity has been inventive.

Because too often discussions of religious belief are lost in antagonistic argument and unthinking hostility and mutual rejection, I hope it is clear, that while arguing as the atheist I am, I do not think that others *must* agree with me, or that those who retain religious faith are somehow less worthy.

Human search for enlightenment has been chastened by taking account of the evolutionary development of human mental powers. An

---

[2] That an apocalypse came in an unexpected form would be the least of anyone's worries.

old view that placed man in dominant position over even women, indeed of all living creatures[3] by divine fiat allowed an inflated view of human beings. Our species, however, has no immediate and accurate access to knowledge, is fallible and must labour to discover what we can and striving for truth we must accept that further learning will correct us.

Certainty as a goal in seeking knowledge is discussed, as is virtual reality. Political questions about democracy and the secular state are canvassed, as are some issues raised about individual rights and communal responsibilities which have been notable during the 2020 Covid-19 pandemic. Some personal reflections on lessons learnt, brief discussions of fascism in Australia and the nature of philosophy provide a measure of additional variation.

Opinions and arguments are here, but not aggressive dismissal. We need to hear each other's convictions with grace and understanding and think about them. People are often too ready to reject other viewpoints, slow to accept difference.

---

[3] Genesis 1: 26-28, 3:16, 22

SLOW LEARNING

Really, I am not talking about intellectual slowness.

Our history as an evolving species holds an immense detritus of mythology, folk belief and commonly accepted opinions, richly accepted but poorly supported. It took millennia for humans to assemble intellectual tools adequate to farther and revise knowledge. The long tussle between religion and science gives some indication. The engineer's bridge must sustain certain stresses. My point is that there is a fault line in common thinking. A neurosurgeon has to rely on accurate and well-established knowledge, and similarly for many other human decisions. There is a significant, on occasions, critically dangerous difference between actual knowledge and baseless opinion (as well evidenced when an American president advocates quack cures while ignoring medical advice).

I write of myself as a slow learner. In early twenties I was captured by fundamentalist Christianity, drowning in piety, and keen to spread the word. Years followed of theological training and decades of pastoral ministry. During that period, I was increasingly aware of discomfort, a growing mismatch between my piety and my brain. I re-entered university studying especially philosophy since I was aware that I needed critical skills to examine my beliefs. Only after so long a time was I alert to the chasm between opinion, belief and knowledge.

The period between first early adolescent religiosity and when I knew that I had to renounce religious faith now stretched over twenty years. That is slow. So deeply entrenched were belief in metaphysical dualism, the habits and associations of those years, that the later period of these years found me dealing with increasing doubt, and uncertainty. But questioning my beliefs. Akin to

4

brainwashing was the commitment to faith: beliefs alien to feelings are not the issue. The real issue was the power of the effects of my religious beliefs were prone to be ignored until it became clear to me that loyalty to my religion was less honest than confronting the issues raised.

I enrolled for PhD studies in philosophy, and the work of Dr Peter Browne, Principal of Trinity College, Dublin, Bishop of Cork and Ross. Browne was contemporary to Georg Berkeley the philosopher, and Dean Jonahan Swift, author of Gulliver's Travels. Browne was a stout defender of traditional Christianity and wrote prolifically in defence of analogical descriptions of God. I concluded that his efforts were well-meaning but wrong. God is reputedly ineffable and remains so[4]. All that we can scratch at are what traditional doctrines tell us – nothing about God, lots about doctrine.

My distrust is confusion between evidence -based knowledge and the use of myth and folk-beliefs presumption of knowledge.

---

[4] An all-powerful, invisible creator is posited, but left to an individual's imagination by imagined analogies.

A FAULT LINE
IN POPULAR THINKING?

Among the essays in this book are personal reminiscences, and essays including thought about living in the present, perception, illusion, or delusion.

Australian attitudes are examined, too. Racism and *Black Lives Matter* are news. The nation's status as a secular state is under attack from the so-called Christian Right.

A fault line runs through popular thinking. Beliefs are commonly received as truths despite being dependent on traditions or mythology, and less well established in history than is thought.

Some thinkers, as if forgetful of history, imagine they have true and certain absolute knowledge. Wisdom is more than being clever with gadgets. How we respect one another even in difference is more important.

MEA CULPA

Yes, I am guilty, I have expressed my beliefs, but have not pursued arguments forcefully, not wishing to aggrieve religious sensibilities. Not overcome by guilt, but uneasy to have complied when exposure was needed.

What needs to be said, unmistakeably, is that disagreeing about religious belief is just that. One does not forsake human concern, need not be aggressively hostile, to recognise that religious belief lacks adequate evidence. People are free to believe whatever, to worship as their religion decrees. My disbelief in eternal consequences will not interfere with their dream world. I do not believe that there is a God or that disbelief is a sin.

It is time to be honest about questions of religion. There has been an established custom to respect religious claims to an afforded[5] privileged position in such discussions. Assumption has been made, that the religious argue from a position of truth, and their opponents are required to be respectful, minimally non-confrontational, even apologetic, as they chip away at traditional bastions of certainty. It is not aggressive or dismissive to insist that the truth or falsity of religious belief is an ordinary human judgement, and that any assumption that divine authority supports religious belief is also itself yet another human judgement.

I also recognise that many Christians are not triumphalist, and that the ragged Christian Right often does the faith harm in their readiness to see most of us as candidates for Hellfire. I recognise that their illusory certainty includes other religions (for some, other sects) amongst the great unwashed who do not share their threadbare confidence. Each religion has developed its own culture, not all of which are on treacherous ground when they hope to include cultic practices or

---

[5] Perhaps they forget all the other religions?

7

sectarian moralities expresses religious faith or belief. Proponents of religious freedom are on uncertain ground in some such claims about freedom.

It would be prudent if the reader viewed the Bible as a purely human collection of books. Not as "the Word of God" as it is often known, but as a collection of ancient writings expressive of religious beliefs and tribal lore. Man, as a special creation having dominion over the earth will not do. The story told by Charles Darwin and others is that humans developed over aeons long before they had developed ways of learning about their world or themselves. We still live in a serious fault line regarding information. On one hand humans have developed knowledge based on evidence. Recognising human fallibility, we eschew claims to final, absolute knowledge and accept that what we know is subject to future experience. On the other hand, the ancient traditions and mythologies are allowed to stake claim to knowledge. So folk-beliefs, religions, communal traditions are awarded credence well beyond their evidential support.

We will explore such questions.

LIVING NOW

NOT NOW AND THEN

A honeybee meanders on the breezes, alighting then soaring off to find other flowers After manoeuvres said to indicate directions to other bees, the bee returns to its home hive. That is "living for the moment" no doubt. But why *this* flower, not leaves of those bushes? Instinct? Some natural distinction between nectar and resting place? Is that knowledge? Does it involve what we would call thinking?

Then there are those animals who gather and store caches of food, build nests. Some hollow out dens, and others even labour to impede streams with log dams. Looking to the future? Some frequently recognise particular people, are familiar with specific places. The owners of some domestic pets are not in doubt, nor are dolphin watchers. Seagulls by the beachside gather expectantly when visitors pause for lunch and swoop for any morsel offered or unwittingly available. So, many creatures utilise their nervous systems to reach goals and achieve purposes, even to cooperate to hunt in packs.

In such ways, it seems obvious enough that purposive actions show how false a traditional view is that only humans think and learn. There is no reason to doubt (we admit readily) that many living species other than human share numerous abilities which humans associate with thinking and remembering. Some less, some more the capacities of non-human species are limited.

Human evolution yielded advantages. It developed a central nervous system which included brain complexity. This afforded the species powers of thinking beyond immediate requirements for survival and nurture. Humans gained a sense of self, identity, consciousness and

9

expanded mental abilities. Metacognition *became* possible, as did extensive memory and language capacity. Over eons the species imperfectly developed social groups and began fallibly to learn about the world and each other, beginning a seemingly endless process.

We are exhorted to live in the present. The past is done if not dusted and the future is unknown to us, yet to be. We are advised to live – in the NOW.

Without question we must be focussed on a present situation, attentive to detail of a task in hand, or alert if the situation could harbour threats. "Single mindedness" becomes necessary when we do need to be "in the present," as in negotiating one's driving through traffic. Or in playing tennis. Or threading a needle. Maybe in reading, playing a violin, assessing a student's response to an assignment or dealing with some family crisis for one's children. We find frequent need to give maximum attention and thought to present concerns. Sometimes we are badly remiss if attention is perfunctory.

We should savour the experiences of life, to enjoy the moment finding fulfilment and satisfaction. To confront life's difficult moments with courage and confidence, times of infirmity or grief with emotion and care and compassion. There will be moments when relationships matter intensely, narrowing our attention and efforts to the present situation and particular people. Treasured memories of sad or joyful times influence our future attitudes and approach to what may befall us.

Well, yes, *living* now, focussing on immediate concerns – does not rob the past of memories and learning, or make our future an aimless lottery.

Ruminating over past events, nurturing grudges, or stressing one's self over past mistakes or failures are all distracting obsessions with the past. "If only ..." regrets for past decisions rarely remedy them. Pedantry about history might well be in the same class. There are such ways to regret indulging some urge to look over one's shoulder. So, there are ways of living in the past to be avoided.

But humans have enlarged capacities in memory and can learn from previous successes and failures, can remember conversations. Memory includes learning of the consequences of earlier choices. Past experiences can guide present actions, or moderate thought too carelessly considered. Our past can moderate our present, to save us from rash words and actions – but should never subdue our spontaneity or creativity. Past ills had better not blight present living.

The future similarly affords opportunities for mesmeric inattention to more pressing matters, even to procrastination regarding perhaps more immediate concerns. Daydreaming about some idealised fantasy, or "castles in the air," wish planning, does not usually translate into achievement. Advice to attend to today's reality at such times might be cogent. Hope is important but hope divorced from reality holds only illusion.

Once again, our mental capacities enable prudent thought about preparation for future projects, needs in old age, for "what if ...?" consideration of likely futures or surprising disasters. Without losing the present to the future, and aware that we lack omniscience, we can consider what consequences our decisions and actions might incur.

Not avoiding situations when "being in the moment" is clearly necessary. We should live more our complex lives with more awareness of past and future than bothers any frivolous butterfly.

Living only for present moments may possibly yield a lifestyle of aimless satisfaction, fleeting opportunities, and emotions, but *it inevitably shapes the future*. There is more to enlarged mental capacities than awareness of the moment.

DILEMMAS

Once a committed Christian clergyman, training and practising for a decade and a half, I renounced faith and have lived thereafter an atheist. Earlier books discuss my thinking about this transition, and I have no wish to elaborate here.

Many others have had similar decisions to make, and I imagine that none have made similar renunciations lightly, so radical are such changes in attitudes, beliefs, and life.

What I seek in this essay is to expose some of the dilemmas which attended my passage from religious faith to contentment as a non-believer. I do not imagine that the experience of others mirrors my transition but feel sure that sharing will be useful.

There was no "magic moment" for me. It was not like flicking a light switch. A process of years saw the adolescent certainties of youth grow into determined commitment and much study. A great deal of questioning fuelled by my studies and arose also in consequence of experiences as a Parish minister. A regular duty, preparing sermons for worship services, meant that I needed constantly to think about my words, conscious that I must represent the faith. But I could not be blind to questions generated by study and by life, amidst the lives and deaths of parishioners. Issues of integrity loomed: initially when adolescent fundamentalist fervour came to terms with realisation that the Bible is not infallibly factual. Jonah emerging still conscious and lucid after a time spent in a great fish's intestines, for just one example.

Christianity is no monolith, no clear body of belief. Around some basic theistic agreement lies a complex array of denominations and sects, a spectrum of beliefs from rigid fundamentalism through liberal theology to vague spiritualism and all-singing all-dancing emotionalism.

The dilemma of choice is solved easily for some, either by ethnic origin or family religion. For these, their faith is often automatically that to which they were born, and many raise no questions. "Other Christians do not know the truth as *we* do: they must be wrong." Other religions than Christianity are believed mistaken, or "pagans do not know the Bible truths".

For many others, however, religious faith presents dilemmas because it is itself complex. The doctrines, liturgies, are many. Some are troubled by modes of dress, moral codes, allowable or forbidden behaviours or amusements. A few fellow students in a Baptist Theological College, would on occasion smoke a cigarette, or enjoy an alcoholic drink in secret while perhaps feeling guilty. The range of doctrines leaves many chinks of opportunity for specific doubts, especially in such areas as attitudes to Scripture, specific tenets, or behaviours. But questions of life after death, eternal punishment, existence of Satan, are amongst dogmas questioned by those in doubt. Thomas the Doubter has many companions.

I had reached conviction that I could no longer preach sermons implying that I believed aspects of Church doctrine, although it had been my duty to uphold them. I was still theist, in some sense Christian. Increasingly I felt I faced this dilemma: I had good relationships with my parishioners, was not in conflict with the Church generally, and believed useful my work in counselling people and supporting them in difficult times, or facing bereavement and the like. But I felt my integrity threatened. I was more an exponent of humanist values than what it is commonly called "a God botherer" might be. I resolved the dilemma by asking to be released from ordained status and I resigned from the Church and my Parish. My view was (and is) that taking the role of clergyman implied that I was a believer and I knew that my beliefs by that time were not those expected of the clergy.

As the time of my resignation from Parish ministry approached, I discussed my dilemma with an Anglican clergyman with whom I was quite friendly, whose Parish was influential. His immediate response came as a surprise. It was that he agreed with my doubtful views, said he shared them, but remained in Christian ministry because his work was socially valuable in that it met personal needs in an acceptable to the community. I did not doubt the value of his work with people but found difficult to believe that that the formal aspects of his work were consistent with his maintaining beliefs which he now expressed. I respected his decision: he was a worthy man. I could not solve my dilemma in that way.

Dilemmas were manifest earlier in other ways. One at the time was disturbing. I was responsible for the liturgy at a service to consecrate a newly built church. A group of other clerics from the same presbytery though that the liturgy was unacceptable and raised charges of heresy which were pursued through the Church's General Assembly. I defended against the charge. My accusers were conservative, tending towards fundamentalist views. The Assembly dismissed the charge of heresy when I revealed that the very words which excited my accusers were part of the liturgy John Knox used. Knox in 1560 led the reformation of the Scottish church. A dilemma arose in going about normal duties, because of differences about nuances of doctrine between clergy.

A great friend over some years was a gifted professional man, extremely active in another congregation, a loyal serving lay member of his Church. He was not a conformist. He organised lessons and carols for Advent, conducted a church choir, and served on denominational committees. I remember occasions in his home when Bach's chorales dominated the house due to his amplifier, and one of his guests roamed the house singing along *auf Deutsch*. His life seemingly balanced all interests, but no dilemma intruded: perhaps not charged with clergy duties, he felt less pressure. Dilemma, I say, not despair. Life's journey reaches many forks along the way, sometimes real crossroads. One makes decisions as well as one can, but as other essays examine guided by to the best evidence available.

THE PEOPLE YOU MEET

Parish work holds an education: the people one meets. Each congregation introduces new faces, different viewpoints, eccentricities, occupations, amongst its members. One meets support, and opposition, disagreement, and rejection. One becomes familiar with mediating between those with different opinions. Dealing with individuals of all ages in so many differing situations spurs one to tolerance and to listen, to wait until one has some understanding of another's situation. One learns that another's initial bonhomie may conceal distress, that unctuous words sometimes disguise petty disagreements. Learning that one is not always right induces new humility. One's acquaintance may also include some with problems one has not previously encountered. One meets as well impressively capable and amiable people whose helpfulness and welcoming openness is a joy.

Some learning leaves scars. In early days, a Parish out of the city had me as a student, weekend "fill in" preacher. A middle-aged woman, not usually at the Church complained of lizards deep in her throat and was acting oddly. I was troubled and struggling to comprehend but realised that she was mentally ill, and also that I was entirely out of my depth. She needed professional help which was well outside my knowledge or ability. The result of my attempt to link her to suitable care is unknown as I was there only as an occasional visitor and had no regular contacts to follow up. That is itself tragic. I had suddenly met with rampant mental illness, and my response was most amateurish and inept.

The incident I remember as my failure. I realised my need for preparation in ways of finding appropriate help when I was confronted with such novel problems. It firmed my resolve to be trained in counselling, as I was for a year by Dr Bruce Peterson, a Sydney psychiatrist in one-to-one tutorials as part of my study at Theological College.

In another Parish later my acquaintance included a paediatric surgeon, who has remained a friend. We are both now retired and have shared our histories of youthful involvement with fundamentalist beliefs. In that parish were those from a wide slice of the local community members some forward looking, others very conservative. Part of my time was mediating a tension between these: I needed extra skills, more tolerance and especially, to take care with any proposal for change: I needed to learn to be patient and to respect people's difference.

Another gave me some insight into the plight of adults living with developmental disabilities, and a glimpse into the sacrifices accepted by those who are their care for them. Visits to hospitals and mental institutions called for sensitivity and insight, not just cheery greetings, or unwanted proselytising. A Church Home for Children was in one Parish, in another.

One lesson I learnt only slowly. Once I answered the door of the Manse to be affected by the sight of my poorly dressed caller, somewhat bedraggled, who seemed less than sturdy. Their approach made much of their indigent family's state and an account of woes. Would I be so kind as to help with some cash so that they that day could eat? Aware that although my stipend was not such as promoted extravagance, I was secure, comfortably housed, and not hungry. I produced the requested money feeling glad to have shared with someone in need. The lesson emerged when I talked with other local clergy from the various denominations. Several of the neighbourhood clergy spoke of a person described just as I remembered who had also visited the other local clergy residences with the plea I so well remembered on that day. Our needy friend had gathered quite an amount as one of my fellow contributors remarked. The lesson: that worthy helping of those in need required that I was careful to know that I let my "heart bleed" when need was genuine. Perhaps taking more time to visit or engage my caller was required, to confirm what I had been told and to be available more wholeheartedly.

The people I met throughout my time in the Church were so varied, such a mixture of personalities and situations and at significant times in their lives, were change agents for me as I grew from the young city lad from a peaceful seaside suburb through the experiences of so many, and so varied people. Many were admittedly passing incidents or formal occasions, but there were many who confided in me, and talked about themselves and their joys and problems, fears, and doubts.

I recanted when my religious beliefs changed, and the course of my life was altered, but I remain indebted to so many people who taught me so much and forgave me the smug certainties that my faith and also my clergy position gave me in those days.

MY TEACHERS

Learning while working by working with people broadened experience and developed some skills not part of my school learning, but other memories are of some who were formally my instructors, at school and elsewhere. Often what comes to mind is not the detail of lesson content, rather their manner and my response at the time. Years have passed and few who taught me are still alive, but I although I remember most names, of even an Infants School teacher, they remain anonymous. The content of their lessons has had whatever effect on the person I am, but I can recall little detail. A few were to be remembered for their less than endearing natures.

My first formal teachers as I began Manly West public school included a warm and welcoming woman which is all I remember other than her name. Primary school began with a male teacher, rotund and insistent about reading, writing and arithmetic. Reasonable but direct. I do remember his solemn advice, that if our bladders demanded relief we should, having sought permission, answer the call lest disaster would follow. The name is all I recall of the somewhat grim man who taught basic subjects the following year, and the relief that end of year meant that my next instructor was an older man, amiable and approachable, whose lessons were delivered more conversationally: he considered his preadolescent pupils to be human. For the final primary year, the Headmaster, newly arrived at this school, was my teacher. Reserved and formal, my only recall is that as part of his duty he made recommendations about the high school his pupils would attend. His choice resulted in the next phase in my development as he nominated me to a secondary school[6].

---

[6] His reasoning? Not for any reason related to me schoolwork or interests, but because my father was a motor mechanic, whose business was favourably received locally.

An old school, begun as Greenwood's school and named for the respected teacher who founded it, had later become an public intermediate high school, which was then elevated by the Education Department to become one of the competitive high schools, and appropriately staffed. Now North Sydney Technical High School, it was situated close to the Northern approaches to the Sydney Harbour Bridge. For the next five years I travelled by bus and tram to school. It was during war time, a brick air raid shelter in the grounds.

No longer class teachers, our instructors taught in their subject disciplines. You do not need, certainly would not want a tedious listing. But some are memorable. In early years there, a teacher of French who used to roam the classroom with book in hand, using it to stimulate attention by striking the back of head of any inattentive pupil. Another of his colleagues was known for occasional appearances asking if anyone might be able to find some hard to buy article because of war shortages. Then there was a mathematics teacher with whom I learnt a lot, but whose temper was fierce. His characteristic form of address was "you silly Sammies!" and he was apt to enforce discipline with a cane. I saw him once cane a classmate quite violently, six strokes on each hand. Then, in a school for easily amused adolescent boys, one female teacher was unremarkable save for the misfortune of initials V.D. One teacher, well advanced in years, was nicknamed Crusty by irreverent students despite his good nature, and known to doze off on occasion, to be waken as the sound of "Crusty" grew from a whisper to disturb his slumber. One science teacher was commander of the school cadet corps, prominent during those war years, no doubt preliminary training for those who would predictably be conscripted if hostilities continued.

There were others, less memorable for such reasons.

I was grateful in later years for lessons in wood and metalwork (I was never expert), and for being introduced to technical drawing. Life changing experiences came there. I met classical music and choir singing, to become a life-long satisfaction. Two music teachers would play recorded works beginning with pieces like "Night on Bare Mountain" or Ravel's "Bolero". They introduced us to music reading and took groups to orchestral concerts. They cultivated a choir, training us in four parts and practising assiduously. I can remember Remembrance Day concerts in the Sydney Town Hall, the school choir crowding the platform and singing to the large audience. In those days imitation poppy petals were released from the ceiling during the ceremony.

Another important influence came again from English teachers who followed each other in my later years at the school. They taught not only the books set for the Leaving Certificate, we were introduced to reading widely in other works, encouraged to read other authors and to collect information, even to gather a scrapbook. I remember the class practising and performing a Shakespeare play, costumed appropriately and even practising fencing with foils. As a result, I read very widely in those years of late adolescence.

Choir singing continued at Teachers College, where we had the opportunity to join the Hurlstone Choral Society in performing Handel's Messiah. A gifted young woman introduced us to educational thinking much more refreshing than my experience at school. More advanced, I must say, than teaching I observed in the schools to which I was appointed.

Piety then overtook me, and I was admitted to Theological studies. Those who stood before classes were often more pious than academic. Some learning was valuable: a year-long one-on-one course on counselling was taught carefully by a psychiatrist, an amiable and erudite retiree lectured New Testament Greek, and annual brief visits from an interstate visitor teaching about Archaeology opened an interest in the speculations about the Dead Sea scrolls. One greatly respected lecturer was referred to as "Professor", not his formal title: a gentle, aged man given to mysticism and piety, adept at avoiding questions to which if frank response were given might have offended conservative listeners. Others took time but were not memorable contributors to my understanding. One other, a visiting clergyman, had been named by students "the man with the muck rake" due to the colourful stories which instruction in pastoral work included.

My learnings at this first brush with theological training were to influence my future thinking, because it taught me that fundamentalism is an aberrant version of Christianity, I came to disrespect the hierarchy with which I needed to deal, I thought unjust the treatment of a student who expressed disbelief that Jonah had survived intact a lengthy ingestion by a great fish. I had learnt to disbelieve the claim that the Bible was inerrantly factual. In a later time at St Andrews Theological Hall I met a Professor of Theology and others whose demeanour and scholarship I respected, even as I was ceasing to share their beliefs.

University studies towards a degree began when I was aged thirty. I was parish minister, studied part-time and late into the night. The Newcastle University was not at first established: its beginning as a remote College of other universities reached establishment while I studied, and my graduation was amongst the first from the new University. The head of the Philosophy group in the Department of Arts was friendly but his teaching was only little less obscure than his miniscule handwriting. I am grateful that he was otherwise most helpful. Later as Professor in the newly formed Philosophy Department I was the sole honours student and listening to his lecture to me in his study I more than once succumbed to sleep, and awoke to see him still on his feet while looking doubtfully at my drooping head but continuing the lecturing. He was my supervisor for PhD studies. Helpful in the process of selecting a topic, when it came to my writing a thesis, his handwritten comments on my drafts were of such obscurity that I soon came to ignore them and just continued to write. Later he employed me, after I left the Church.

During this study in the new institution I met others. A philosopher steeped in European classics but overlaid with a veneer of Andersonian realism following study in Sydney. My first teacher in formal logic was John Anderson's son, who (I later learnt when I came across a copy of his father's logic course notes) was a faithful son. I came to think that he would have flourished had he followed his interest in literature, rather than his father's path. My first teacher in German was a German woman, who related well to students, and was careful to make the course as far as possible one that immersed us in the language and minimised laborious translation.

I also met a young Melbourne man whose scholarship to Cambridge transformed him into a very model of an eccentric Cambridge classicist. The man who led the nascent university was a graduate of Trinity College Dublin, had experience in Egypt and with British intelligence (I think) in troubled times. He later became Vice Chancellor left his mark on the developing university. His successors have not always had his full and rounded view of the University's task.

My teachers have been significant in educating me, perhaps more often as by the effect of their personalities and manner of interacting with others than by the formal content of their teaching. Some have taught me unintentionally not to share their attitudes or behaviours. Some learning concerns ways of being one should avoid. On the other hand, memories of interested and committed educators who relate and communicate well have set goals that I hope to achieve.

BRUISER

We will use his nickname. I was aged twenty-one, a teacher in a small central western town, new to the role in the second year after college. Bruiser was in an upper primary class, about ten years old, nuggetty. He had the distinction that he was the only Catholic child in the central school: nuns at the convent school had seen him off to the public school – too big a handful.

His family background was not fashionable or affluent, nor prominent in the town. Bruiser was talkative, well versed in the vernacular, always ready with a quick retort. He was brighter than had been realised, affable and quick if he was interested. His reputation as a difficult pupil was not consistent with the boy who appeared in my class.

Bruiser was an able student, no laggard but not the most eager. He was cheerful and memorable, an inquisitive young lad. His writing, careless and awkward, was left-handed and at the time it was fashionable to insist that the proper manner of writing was right-handedly. Amiable as he was, Bruiser's response to compulsion was careless, a non-cooperative silent submission. His writing improved when I sat with him and took a pen in my left hand and practised writing with him in that fashion.

At times I had wondered what his earlier experience had been, or whether perhaps he had need for defences because of harsh treatment at home or elsewhere. Apart from class time contact I had no window on his circumstances. But it is interesting that he still stands out as memorable when those past decades have washed other memories away. He seemed not too conscious of the past, and I did not see that he gave much thought to the future, but he surely lived in the present with determination and vivacity.

Arriving at the school a little early one morning I was greeted enthusiastically as Bruiser accosted me. "Sir, Sir, Come see what I've got!" I followed his way to the classroom, amused and curious at his excitement. A cardboard carton by my desk was his goal. "Look, Sir, look." He tipped the carton and suddenly, I watched a released echidna[7] scamper about the classroom. We spent some brief time since he was so proud to have produced this spectacle, and that he had achieved the near impossible capture and containment of this fascinating spiny creature. I was moved by his wanting to share his excitement with me and took delight in his sense of triumph and achievement. Then we carefully recaptured the by now terrified monotreme and released it in nearby bushland.

There have been times over the years when I have wondered what lay ahead of him, but distance and time, as well as the task of living my own experience, have precluded finding answers. Besides, it is *his* life, but for me only curiosity and nostalgia for the fresh times of youthful learning. So many, pupils in schools I taught, parishioners, decades of students in philosophy, and other students: lives touched but not for me to follow.

Memories I still have, not panoptic, but the privilege of playing a role in their life adventure does not give me any licence to intrude on their history or their privacy. That is why Bruiser has remained nickname only.

---

[7] A spiny anteater, *Tachyglossus.*

INDIVIDUALS in SOCIETY

Some significant controversies are distorted because the underlying argument is between what is known, evidence-based, on one hand, and folk beliefs, often traditional but unsupported by good evidence.

Entrenched folk belief not supported by sound evidence corrupts much public and policy thinking, and affects personal attitudes, even promotes expectations of apocalyptic scenarios ending world events. This issue was prominent in 2020 during the pandemic due to the coronavirus in initial responses by President Donald Trump in the United States of America, who dismissed as "like the flu, will disappear as in a miracle quite quickly" the pandemic which has cost well over 150,000[8] American lives.

Public Health practitioners urged isolation of contacts, and social distancing restrictions against mass gatherings. There was then a clamour from some groups rejecting restrictions on personal contact in groups on grounds that personal freedoms are sacrosanct.

This arose because a popular and fiercely protected American value[9] in individual freedom was assumed to deny any restriction on individual freedom of movement and association. It was argued that personal freedoms overrode even well-advertised personal advice to avoid social contacts leading to infection of others by Covid-19. The outcome: whether attendance at political rallies, protest demonstrations or religious gatherings or even because of isolation-induced disruption

---

[8] This figure was exceeded by 30 July 2020.
[9] The Land of the Free.

of socialising habits large gatherings assembled, and community contact ensured that the cases of the Covid-19 in America rose.

That reaction calls for an answer.

It indicates an unresolved conflict between individual freedom and collective responsibility. If there is conflict about such matters, is evidence based knowledge to govern responses or should individual opinion or loyalty to emotional slogans decide? But to answer that affirming individual freedoms are primary is to ignore individual responsibilities incurred by membership in a community (or family, for that matter)[10].

Firstly, appeal to the Constitution is vain. Government legislation limits individual action in many ways. The law condemns trespass, renders various Government sites off limits, prevents random visits to defence establishments and the like. Argument that civil rights are infringed by government limiting individual rights of movement and assembly when dealing with fatal results of a pandemic seems frivolous. But the USA fiercely protects private gun ownership, with at least a hint of historical nostalgia for armed civilian militias able to oppose unwanted government actions. One suspects that embers of the Civil War still glow.

Those stridently claiming individual rights should consider responsibilities which flow from belonging to a society and recognise that their fellows also have rights. At the least, other citizens ought not be harmed by an individual's actions. Wantonly engaging in crowd activities, knowing the risk of infection, or of being carrier of infection, is a deliberate risking of the welfare of the individual's fellows. *Determined to risk infection with a fatal disease, and to risk causing*

---

[10] Often overlooked, even the Biblical ten commandments stress social issues, for those interested. The Christian Right, powerful in USA, would see the Bible as overriding government legislation.

others being infected, is to ignore the individual's responsibility of care for others.

CENSORSHIP IS NOT AN EASY ANSWER

A response I have heard to such situations is that everyone is entitled to whatever opinion they reach, but that their opinion is not to be influential *unless it is true.* That is, it must not be just someone's opinion without substantial evidence, a reasonable remark. For this solution, however, difficulties quickly emerge. How is truth to be established authoritative? Who is to decide about truth? As a quick indication of the problem let me introduce a case which indicates why such questions matter.

Not so long ago (as history goes) there was a time in Europe when truth was determined by consistency with Christian teaching. An institution in those times known as the Inquisition tried, even torturing or executing any who ventured a divergent opinion. The truth was as the church (or those in power in the church) declared. In those circumstances, opinion was rejected if thought not true. Variant views on Christian belief earned the martyrdom of heterodox Christians. Christian belief was believed true beyond question, guaranteed by God. The Church is not these days believed competent to enforce its opinions.

Legislative decisions about truth are similarly fallible. As are any other potential authorities: none is competent to adjudicate claims that an opinion is true. Notable is government denial of climate change despite overwhelming agreement amongst climate scientists.

Truth is claimed when appropriate tests are not failed when adequate to the question and rigorously pursued. We are always in the position that the history of human thought (including science) demonstrates fallibility. As we learn, our decisions about what is true remain conditional upon not meeting experiences revealing that we have been mistaken. Some beliefs in medicine, in the physical sciences, in social matters have endured for centuries until advancing knowledge taught us that what we believed was complex in ways we had not understood.

This is no disaster. Knowledge has not collapsed into random chance or haphazard guesses about cause and effect. Realising that human thought is fallible, that learning is a continuous project does not negate what we do know. It frees us from illusions that absolute, final truths are realistic goals for our efforts. The delusion that immaterial non-human sources of wisdom and truth reveal their riches when they are ready is a fantasy[11].

There are frequent conflicts, obviously, between individual needs and opinions and the social needs and opinions of the individuals' community.

We have no difficulty in recognising that individuals would lose most freedoms if their entire lives were communally controlled, or even if individual matters were directed by community functionaries. We hardly need to learn that individual liberties and choices, goals and relationships are not for civil authorities to control. Much history recounts struggles to achieve individual liberties[12] and there is an amount of legislation favouring them.

There remains much to be done to ensure that those luxuriating in individual freedoms find a more equal recognition of their responsibilities to members of their communities. The reaction mentioned above, against social distancing during the coronavirus

---

[11] How many millennia has it taken, for extra-terrestrial information from immaterial sources to emerge? One suspects that a worthier extra-terrestrial source might be more informative.

[12] Some cultures maintain more rigid social controls, and pockets of discrimination remain in societies boasting freedom.

pandemic is the case in point which sparked these ruminations. One imagines that a duty of care for fellow citizens would be demonstrated by limited free association and gathering closely even for praiseworthy causes, thus avoiding exposure of large numbers of people to possibly fatal infection[13]. Indeed, one would have thought that so obvious that even freedom-loving citizen would have wondered about deciding to make precaution a priority.

---

[13] Not considering the individual concerned self-interested risk avoidance of infection

MORALITY

Morality has occupied human ingenuity since before written history. Standards of morality, prescriptions and forbidding are varied in the differing religions and cultures.

Although its comfortable assumptions have supported many, the Judeo-Christian tradition arrived reasonably late in the evolution of human civilisation. The moral codes developed by Hebrews and later in Christianity have never been universal. Those who do not subscribe to the religions of Judaism or Christianity, or who are atheist, do not see those codes as basic, or universally binding.

Human beings evolved, we believe initially in Africa, but early groups of protohumans settled over time in diverse places, some isolated. In various places, as societies formed language became communication and living in communities developed, living with others presented challenges for which some agreement had to be reached by whatever means could be devised. The group living of primates gives some idea of such beginnings.

What this implies is that despite common religious beliefs, morality does not stem from non-human commands, but from the desires and needs confronting early humans as the red in tooth and claw methods of untamed animals were replaced by pressures of survival and comfort. The "law of the jungle" was inadequate. Cooperation sufficient to enable group coexistence to be more peaceful meant rethinking interactions and relationships. Protocols developed amongst groups into what we now think of as ethics or morals to meet their situations, not by consulting some manual of universal correct behaviours.

Inhabitants of what is today known as Australia developed a culture which had rules about clan membership, marriage with means of avoiding in-breeding, limits to retribution, and similar[14]. So did inhabitants of other isolated regions. As populations massed, various others found part of their developing cultures ways of believing and acting which later became religions in more well-known of today's form. These were communally stabilising and formalised their local views of morality. In early days for humanity, these were often believed enforced by the command of local deities. Formalised expressions of such religions are still with us.

The Ten Commandments of the Bible's Old Testament exemplify the process. The ten begin with commands relating to Hebrew religion (No other Gods, Day of Worship, No blasphemy), and the remainder are to do with social living (Tell no lies, Do not kill, Don't covet, Marriage). But the restriction on killing was compatible with genocidal elimination of non-
Hebrew tribes by divine command. Or transgressors of various social rules.

This is similar in other cultures, other religions, with allowances for cultural variations. But common themes concern sexuality, marriage in particular[15], gender matters including homophobia. Moral matters are convoluted: they are related to differing cultures, and cultures at various times. The Bible's New Testament modifies many of the rules of the Old.

Not to labour the point tediously, morality is not a matter of Divine Command, or religious obligation. And moral codes are human inventions, answers to social living, fallible, worthy of thoughtful review and not laws against which eternal destinies are decided.

---

[14] British invaders did not notice or understand the communal structures and laws of Indigenous Australians.

[15] With differences, for example the Old testament entertains polygamy, as does Islam.

Morality is in the situation that we have already considered. It is a human concern. It must rest on human thinking and social challenges. It is not a matter of Divine decrees.

Without enlarging the issue here, it is relevant to notice that the Ten Commandments, as also the beatitudes of Jesus, prominent moral sources
in much religious teaching, are *not* especially ethical. In both cases behaviours are offered reward for achievement, or punishment for nonachievement for observation. That is an appeal not to morality, but to self-interest. All too often, today's values are centred on individual satisfactions, when (like the social commandments amongst the Ten despite their appeal to self-interest) the consideration is on living with care for the needs of others.

Humans are fallible, more intelligent or less, more or less aware of others, sometimes careless and sometimes dismissive of consequences for others. Some think that freedom implies that they have no obligations to not risk the welfare of others, some value being wealthy and have only disparagement for the needy. So moral codes are only part of humanity's response to the pressures of communal living. Law is needed since some do not respect moral constraints. Another mechanism lies in etiquette, a way of smoothing social interaction less severe than criminal law and modifying behaviours without crying moral judgement.

Morality is important, because living amongst people is our way, and humans cannot satisfy all their inclinations and desires unless some ways are devised to ensure that the freedoms involved are mutual. We attempt to live with reciprocal respect and not to the detriment of others.

TRUE?

We humans have acted as if the Judeo-Christian scriptures were right to describe humans as created in God's image[16]. So certain that truth was at our command, that *a priori* arguments could truly reveal even the existence of God, and that dominion over the earth and its creatures was unlimited.

Darwin was amongst the early thinkers who developed the correction of evolutionary theory, which has cast new light on human origins. Humans are no longer thought of as images of God, to be honest, thinking humans do not think much about the concept of a God these days.

The extended history of human learning about our world, about being human and living peacefully with others, the aberrations in development, wars and pestilence seem to underline the difficulty of our slow attainment of what knowledge and sagacity we have reached.

But while humans have talked about truth, have even gone to war to defend what was believed true, and philosophers joined other thinkers in the search for finally true knowledge, we have come to recognise that we can be mistaken. It took humans a long time to come to realise that fallibility challenged the certainties flowing from belief that they were like God and the world was their dominion. No "special creation" they evolved from simple life forms, as other species did, and do. So many creeds, so many martyrs, so many religions, so many polities.

---

[16] Feuerbach insightfully corrected this: "man first unconsciously and involuntarily creates God in his own image" *The Essence of Christianity,* p. 118. It is difficult to see how "image" is an appropriate description of man, given that God is immaterial and ineffable, though all usual references to God seem like man grown infinitely large and wise.

But here, at last, we learn that today's truth may correct what we thought true yesterday, and that tomorrow may cause us yet again to reconsider. Even our account of history is subject to inaccuracy – written by the victors, as it is said, the voices of the vanquished are often suppressed, and the gilding of the lily of success is not unknown.

Consequently, care that knowledge should be claimed only if based on sound evidence, and not merely on mythology or traditional folk belief is necessary. Some essays amongst those in this book are at pains to argue this.

Distinguishing truth from error, recognising untruth parading as reality, exposing deception remains essential. That is not in doubt. We do know when it is safe to cross the road, we avoid sources of infection, we have learnt how to act if someone is injured. Knowledge of our earth and its surrounding space is accumulating, and technologies of communication and engineering produce wonders. There is no doubt that we learn, and trust our learning, just as surely as we also have a history of mistakes and have still learning ahead of us.

But our concept of truth can no longer be that what we recognise now as truth is absolute, complete. We do not know whether future experience may show a certainty to be false, whether we have come to a new learning.

What we do know is that truth is not attained cheaply by pretending, however we might speculate about matters concerning us, truth is not so reached. A slick answer might comfort and perhaps quieten us momentarily but leave us still wondering. To depend on beliefs supported by persuasive rhetoric or popular opinion but which are lacking solid support is no safe path to knowledge or truth.

KNOWLEDGE PRESSUMED OR REAL

FOLK BELIEFS

Tradition, mythology, sometimes familiar habit are the unsustained origins of many popular beliefs. Of these beliefs a number intrude detrimentally on society.

Although widely accepted, these bases for belief lack evidence of truth. It will be convenient here to use "folk belief" as a term embracing varieties of legend and other unproven convictions, or traditional speculative "best guesses."

Folk beliefs may be remnants of early attempts to explain problems which were then beyond human knowledge[17], often raising metaphysical questions. Folk theories and mythologies are powerful relics of ancient puzzles – but are no substitute for evidence-based learning. Presumed in beliefs they do not warrant being taken as *knowledge*. We explore this difference.

Folk beliefs are many and some have little significance like "it is unlucky to walk under ladders" or "black cats presage disaster." Where would we be without innocent foibles? As with fiction, dream boats and castles in the air, people are free to roam in imagination through non-factual fantasy.

---

[17] Folk beliefs are corrected as knowledge and theories develop. Examples: popular tales of peoples' behaviour became psychology, and popular remedies were superseded by evidence-based medicine. Knowledge replaces folk-guesses in various fields. An early association of fever with the air of swamplands led to naming Malaria (from "bad air") when later knowledge implicated mosquitos, then even later previously unidentified organisms transferred to victims by mosquito carriers were recognised.

Other folk beliefs, however, determine life choices and commitments. Consequential belief demands that evidence supports its truth if it is to be trusted with weighty implications. No belief, however popular, is trustworthy as a basis for significant commitments, unless its own truth is beyond doubt.

It is disturbing that a prominent and powerful politician in today's international affairs seems uncomprehending about the difference between studied knowledge and the recommendations of snake-oil remedies. To our dismay, a prominent American politician deals with serious public health concerns with hillbilly insouciance and prioritises economic issues while death visits vast numbers of people who were advised to ignore medical precautions and to trust dubious, possibly harmful, remedies. This leader of a "great society" despises actual knowledge, preferring folk-wisdom's guesswork, and harbours ill-based suspicion of conspiracy theories alleging that medical doctors working for human health and welfare are agents of nefarious plots detrimental to public good. He is a prominent contemporary example of a prevalent attitude, knowledge ignored in favour of folksy intuition. Narcissistic delusion pitted against serious scholarship.

Large masses of the world's population make the same choice.

Beliefs, traditional but untested, are trusted rather than established knowledge. Entrenched folk beliefs corrupt much pub

lic and policy thinking on social issues, they determine personal attitudes and even promote apocalyptic solutions to world events.

There is an evident fault line[18] through popular attitudes on prominent issues. In matters like engineering bridges or needing

---

[18] Fault line: A Geological metaphor - The San Andreas Fault in California is in an area with c.13 million people. It is possible that earthquake will be serious and destroy much building and infrastructure. Confident human lives and activity are at risk along this fault line. Human beliefs (old, important - not based on established fact, but on

neurosurgical attention or repairing motor engines or technical aspects of trades skills, knowledge is essential. If the question involves religion, or politics and a wide range of behavioural issues, folk beliefs often triumph over information – any opinion can be entertained if supported by folk belief.

KNOWLEDGE from MYTHOLOGY?

On one hand we have knowledge

Mythologies can be known and understood. There we find lessons about attitudes and behaviours to consider, rarely gain knowledge about facts and external reality.

No cosmic encyclopaedia contains a source of all true knowledge. Knowledge beyond mere subsistence is unavoidable to most living beings though we might speculate about what some primates and marine mammals think or know. Any belief that ancient myths and religions taught infallible superhuman truths is delusory. Knowledge is human, the hard-won results of fallible effort. Despite much pious belief there is no non-human font of arcane knowledge.

Human knowledge began early in cognitive evolution as our distant ancestors developed consciousness before *homo sapiens* reached the scene. Many cultures still embrace ancient mythologies which grappled with human ignorance during the period in which consciousness was developing amongst protohumans, amid struggles with communal living as life became more demanding than merely survival and avoidance of predators. Poor, nasty, brutish and short life must have been at the beginnings of socialisation. For that struggle

---

folk beliefs) are a fault line in thinking and have consequences. (Google: San Andreas Faultline facts).

intellectual tools limited to guesswork and superstition had to suffice. There was much to learn in the unforgiving strangeness of competition amongst clans, as pre-humans reached for sustenance and safety. Obvious physical facts that fire burns, wounds hold peril, and water is not to be inhaled were quickly evident while much was still mysterious. Abrupt cacophony in cloudy skies suggested expressions of rage by powerful sky beings directed at limited human comprehension as life's uncertainties invited speculation. There were mysterious questions which generated speculation but lacked boundaries to imagination.

Life, it has been said, was not meant to be easy.

Evolving consciousness, early in learning about living in social groups faced mediating conflicts about problems of social living that are still with us.

Finally (not so long ago) science[19] assumed its modern status. Science does not pretend to omniscience or infallibility: its pronouncements are subject to correction when experience demands. All human knowledge is "work in progress." And the evolution of humans implies that although we have achieved much, there remains much that humans do not know[20]. We have also made significant mistakes in our theorising and have needed to correct ourselves.

There is no reason to think that humans will ever know *everything*, or that everything that excites human curiosity will be satisfied. There is no reason to believe that human fallibility will be replaced by infallible truths. Early human thinking, primitive ambition

---

[19] From Latin *scientia* (a knowing, knowledge of, acquaintance with, skill in)
[20] We have much to learn about our planet and are constantly learning that our forebears' belief that earth was central to the universe was far too parochial a view. When it was believed that gravity was a force attracting falling objects to earth's centre, we had yet to learn that the cosmos did not centre on human interests.

for "perfect knowledge" found that an *el dorado* of the mind was another wishful delusion.

So, on one hand we have knowledge. What we learn about our world, and ourselves – far beyond the imaginings of our predecessors.

On the other hand, we have mythology and religious belief.

These are fostered by less secure convictions arising from our fallibility. What calls for caution about these notions is that often they are promoted as if they were indeed also knowledge.

Beliefs they are, yes – emphatically – but not knowledge.

This deserves explanation, not least because there is a need to maintain the difference between knowledge and belief. Unquestionably, people can hold whatever opinions, and express their beliefs, emotional responses, and attitudes. But unless established by sound evidence, those opinions remain something *they think*, not a truth to proclaim. Some opinions are no better than vacuous chatter.

Imagine the consequences if our influential politician advocated that domestic bleach or disinfectant be ingested or injected as therapy for some viral infection. If gullible citizens did as the politician advised it might indeed end the viral infection – but by death not by healing. That belief is not knowledge. Similarly, delusional beliefs however treasured and comfortable are not knowledge -- just mistakes.

Political discourse is distorted if folk belief is substituted for knowledge, when seriously damages social decision-making. In earlier times such topics as religion, politics and sex were not polite conversation, while now they are commented on freely. Folk beliefs frequently clash with knowledge in socially undesirable ways: an incomplete list below indicates some obvious areas. A deep silence still enfolds major issues which deserve discussion, firm decision, and resolute remedial action.

Our educational thinking is distorted: Revision of secular educational education should not favour folk beliefs more than actual knowledge and should inculcate human ethics rather than scriptural commands. Education should aim at developing personal skills and attitudes, not be seen primarily as vocational training. Non-government schools should be taxable. The role of universities should concern inquiry and broad education, not mainly vocational preparation. Scholars need to value knowledge and to recognise its devaluation when truth is abandoned for mere opinion.

Other issues depend on views stemming from folk beliefs. Some present areas need to be reviewed in the light of data, instead of being predetermined by traditional opinions. They include status and payment of women, prevalent domestic abuse and violence, the incidence of child abuse. Other matters include gender issues, racism, and jingoistic patriotism. Then there is opposition to vaccination. Politics is the poorer for an apparent preference of folk beliefs and attitudes over evidence-based policy on national security, welfare, and prosperity. International relations seem too often guided by traditional perceptions of alien powers than by data driven calculation. Scientific consensus regarding climate change is denied while political support is afforded for fading fossil fuel energy solutions. Parties strive for popular approval based on individual interests often narrowly conceived in financial terms. Similarly, self-seeking descent of political parties into despicable strategies of conflict and competition for power often neglects national issues of importance. Government reliance on income from gambling and other socially damaging sources, with dependence on motor cars and poor public transport adds to this picture. Another set of issues concerns government relations with churches and their influence. Electoral outcomes are distorted by the presence of demographic groupings favouring large blocks of voters guided by folk belief opinions on religion. Senior Churchmen seem protected from effects legal accountability for paedophilia matters and generally.

CERTAIN ERROR[21]

One can feel **certain**: perhaps, a sense that "I've realised: what I think now *is true.*"

Descartes (1596-1650) an early modern French philosopher remembered also for cartesian geometry famously wrote "*cogito ergo sum*" – "I think, therefore I am." But that certainty dissolved into error.

Descartes held a prior belief that no material being could think. Only immaterial beings, spirits, could think. Descartes' mind, in his view an immaterial being, not his body (a material thing) alone could think. His *prior* belief was in a dualism of mind and body.

The certainty that he was conscious of thinking did not warrant the beliefs about material and immaterial substances involved in the belief he had about himself[22]. So, feeling of certainty can be all too real, yet prove to be an *ignis fatuus,* an imaginative wraith. Historically philosophers had sought certainty in the *a priori*[23] as if some truths were axiomatic independently of human experience. Others not of this mind looked for certainty from their experience of the world, but illusions and

---

[21] A journalistic edited version appeared in The Newcastle Herald on Monday 1 June 2020.

[22] The notion is ancient: myth has traditionally fostered a notion that the material world (changing, impermanent) is accompanied by an immaterial world (variously populated by spirits, gods, demons, post-mortem immaterial humans, etc). The myth is common to much ancient thought and literature and continues to pervade all major religions. Popular as such beliefs are, they remain mythological and lack evidence apart from ancient religious speculations of primeval humans attempting to explain questions developing amongst protohumans before human knowledge began to replace speculative responses to mystification.

[23] *a priori* argument is not based on experience, but on premises assumed true or believed to be axiomatic.

perceptual error undermine conviction that sensory perception simpliciter yields truth. Human fallibility is inescapable.

So humans have to come to terms with their own evolution, as with the evolution of all living things (even coronavirus strains) despite certainties about religious beliefs which led to contempt for Darwin (*et al*), consequences of Mendel's work, and later evolution of the theory of evolution itself.

This divergence of views is a prime example of a continuing conflict between attempts to confront human need to learn about the world and each other, and claims to already have certainty in beliefs fostered mythologically, or those finding certainty and comfort in supposing life after death. Such speculations shielded against fears magnified by lack of knowledge, threat or danger, or illness and mortality.

Because humans evolve this conflict is unsurprising. Our remote ancestors were life forms without language, lacking cognitive abilities and emotional capacities. Social groups, settlements, civilizations were yet to develop (that process continues!). In time early humans had to learn to relate, to communicate, and lacked the methodology and mensuration, the written language and its records, and so speculations and guesswork were at a premium. The known relics of the early cultural beliefs of various ethnic groups remind us with traces of the processes involved. World-wide, there are ethnic groups holding today's forms of earlier religions developed by different peoples.

Depending largely on available levels of communication and education the conflict of beliefs mentioned above is evident in any society having extensive contact with other societies.

There are those who continue to confront uncertainty, questions or doubt by inquiry, experiment, attempting to find answers. There are those who welcome new knowledge, accept change, and curious about what may be possible. Let us call them "fallible enquirers." Slowly, over millennia, there has grown (developing more recently than we imagine) what we have called science, and the methods have developed, mensuration invented, medicine divesting many of its folk-cures in favour of evidence-based practice, and psychology and social sciences attempted to learn about our living in groups and nations. The present writer's father was a young child when the Wright brothers first flew. My father-in-law in later life (toward the end of the 20th century) was surprised by a photograph reproduced on a fax machine. The rate of knowledge increase has been accelerated.

It is not surprising that there are many people in areas not well acquainted with modern processes. There are educationally or socially deprived communities without reason to know about recent learning, people whose way of life has not been disturbed by change. When modernity and the technologies made possible by recent science are not available, intrusion by modernity can be destabilising. Cargo Cults in Papua New Guinea are evidence. But even in societies enjoying (or worried by) the trends of modernity there are many people who do not welcome, maybe do not know, about matter that interest the curious of the preceding paragraph.

A consequence is that in any society there are, as well as our "fallible enquirers," those we might dub the "insecurely certain." Here lies an area of conflict between two different mind-sets. Where the "fallible enquirers" are comfortable with questions yet unresolved and with change consequent on researched answers to problems, the "insecurely certain" want to avoid the uncertainties of doubt or enquiry by adopting beliefs in which they feel certain. But this essay begins by indicating that certainty is an uncertain guide to the truth. Especially when one examines the source of this certainty.

Claiming certainty about beliefs has been a historic boast of those propagating religious belief. However, there are too many religions which do not sing from the same hymn sheet. Indeed, they are often enough mutually hostile. Their foundation narratives and arguments for divine foundation are mutually inconsistent. Their certainties are frequently incompatible. Fallibility (although a human universal) is not recognised. The mythological bases for belief are not usually discussed, even though mythology supports central beliefs. This essay is primarily not about religion, so I have no desire to discuss this at length. Apart from underlining the fragility of claimed certainty here my point is that this is one major area of "insecure certainty."

Another such area lies with the creators and supporters of many conspiracy theories. There are, without doubt, actual conspiracies of various groups, aimed at multitudinous ends. Even, let it be said, in political parties in our own Parliament. No one denies such that such conspiracies form, to whatever effect. Human conspiracies are frequent, some with wide consequences.

These are not the conspiracies to which I refer. Unlikely tales as well are peddled by conspiracy theorists. These are often dark plots, sometimes extreme enough to raise suspicion about the imagined power and cunning of the those creating them. Frequently such conspiracy theories are embraced by individuals whose information is far from complete, who are incapable of action to oppose even a conspiracy at local council level in a development matter, and have no possibility of addressing the issues supposedly raised. At this time (in 2020) the Covid-19 pandemic is occupying the world's attention, and much ink has been spilt refuting a so-called Plandemic conspiracy which promotes blatantly false information possibly damaging to public health. Notoriously, the American Federal answer to the Coved-19 pandemic has in large measure been framed by the President's personal certainties rather than by informed Public Health advice from medical specialists in the field. There are other massive conspiracy theories floated in

American federal politics at present as a Presidential election approaches (Obamagate).

Other alarmist theories see vast international financial conspiracies attributed to a prominent wealthy Jewish family (does this sound familiar?). Conspiracy theories often stem from some happening, or interpret some incident, and then a devious story is crafted which seems believable, if the conspiracy theorist is crafty enough with hearers employing imaginations big enough to outstrip their critical faculties.

Similarly, in respect of race, gender, sexuality, social status, sectarian interest, those nursing a bias and prejudice will often express certainties resting on stereotypes or gossip without any factual basis other than personal dislike or racial fear however learnt. Politics is a rich source of such misplaced certainties. As is any sporting competition.

At its heart the conflict between the "fallibly enquirers" and the "insecure certain" is between those who fully accept their fallibility as humans, and the fact that there is always more to learn, and those whose insecurity cannot be content without a firm belief, one they take to be certain, even if there is no substantial evidence to establish it.

Certainly, the "fallibly enquirers" (including scientists) are human, and so mistakes are possible[24]. But science together with responsible research and peer review is protected by rigorous methodological procedures, designed to reveal mistaken or misleading conclusions. Fallible, yes, but unlike the ready certainties of conspiracy theories, prejudices or guesswork mentioned, science is alert to fault and fraud and active to avoid them.

Whatever their cognitive capacities, humans are often beset by such limiting factors as indifference and sheer laziness. Ready certainties, myths, conspiracy theories, prejudice and fear are easier and lazier than

---

[24] That is what fallible means.

taking the effort to understand a situation, consider how to respond, and what the consequences might entail for others and for one's fellows. Taking comfort by embracing conveniently easy certainties can disappoint when the cost of that comfort is grief or a realisation of one's own fickle thoughtlessness.

DELUSION

Both "an illusion" and "a   " refer to a mistake about reality. Illusion can refer to misperception, such as a mirage, an ambiguous effect of light on one's surroundings or recognising a voice as familiar, only to find that the speaker is not the person one thought. The word is used usually for some perceptual aberration. An illusion can be said to be created, verbally or by perspective, or a creative person might be said to create an illusion verbally, pictorially of a scene or emotion, perhaps. Essentially an illusion is a mental state mistaken about reality.

Delusion[25], its close relative, also refers a mental mistake, involving departure from reality. Delusion often is systematic, long term and acted upon in significant matters without recognition of its departure from reality.

Delusions sometimes are amongst the symptoms of mental illness: perhaps in rumination about evil intent by imagined foes, or feared bodily states, may concern inflated (or underestimated) personal abilities and personal relationships. This essay does not delve into this territory.

Everyday incidents resulting in mistaken affections, suspicion, hostilities, or mistakes are not of interest here. But many folk beliefs are deeply entrenched in popular thinking. Should we think of them as illusions, productive of delusions? Is any widely held belief unsupported by sound evidence illusory or a delusion?

Numerous such common beliefs we are content to treat merely as unproven, but as not leading to dangerous or harmful consequences. If

---

[25] The Shorter Oxford English Dictionary includes "Anything that deceives the mind with a false impression; a deception; a fixed false opinion with regard to objective things." Both words are derived from Latin: illusion from *illusio, mock, jest at*, and delusion from *deludere*, play false, mock.

people express their dislike of others by putting their names in the freezer, we may think them odd, but not likely to be dangerous. If they tread on cracks in pavement, we do not fear for their mothers' spinal health.

Folk beliefs can, though, have, serious consequences for people's decisions and the course of their lives and such require handling with care.

Unproven folk beliefs of such consequence are not so innocent and should at least be examined critically. A presidential belief in 2020 that covid-19 is just another flu which would miraculously disappear within weeks was taken as accurate by many; and believing that an exaggerated view of personal freedom of association justifies risking others, even community infection with the coronavirus are such folk beliefs. The massive fatal effects flowing from such beliefs are powerful reminders that beliefs having such consequences are false.

Similarly, devout prayer for rain, even if such prayer coincides with celestial moisture, are as often as not futile. Beliefs in the power of love, forgiveness and Christian (or Islamic, or other) unity – supported by earnest supplication have seen the growth of thousands of sects of upright true believers who argue with some hostility over supposedly common beliefs.

I have no wish to labour this point here, but given the multiplicity of religions and the dearth of reasons to declare any proved true, is cause to reflect on the possibility that delusion drives religious belief, that the authoritative sources of such belief are illusory

CONTAGEOUS MEMES

Richard Dawkins [26] popularised the discussion of the replication of memes, a useful concept when considering the spread of beliefs.

Memes drive systems of thought. Some spread like pandemics, infecting multitudes Unremarkable in itself, this fast spreading of ideas raises concern when the contagious meme is itself erroneous.

If a meme is infected with error, may become a carrier of that infection, infecting contacts and widespread disinformation may be the result. This metaphor speaks to my concern that folk beliefs including myths are so readily, often quite uncritically, accepted as if they were established truths. Such acceptance is only justified when there are good grounds for belief, and those grounds are a rational decision that the belief is not mere supposition or someone's "best guess." Mere traditional support of belief, or historicity, institutional affirmation, or shamanistic declaration are insufficient.

The world is recipient of numerous religions which are presented as truths concerning such untestable matters as life after death, invisible and immaterial forms of non-human life, regions (presumably in such immaterial locations) devoted to blissful reward for piety, or extreme punishment for the wanton. Many religions claim truth and reject others. Their incompatibility, or their outré assertions, suggest that at most one of these could be true since they are contradictory. But, which one? And

---

[26] Dawkins, Richard, 1989, *The Selfish Gene,* new edition, Oxford, Oxford University Press.: "Examples of memes are tunes, catch-phrases, clothes fashions, ways of making pots or of building arches. Just as genes propagate themselves in thew gene pool by leaping from body to body via sperm or eggs, so memes propagate themselves by leaping from brain to brain via a process which, in the broad sense, can be called imitation," p. 206

why? All, however confident and however devoted their adherents, fail the essential test that there is independent confirmation of their claims. That matter is not to be sidestepped: all religions invoke immaterial beings, many have beliefs in human survival *post mortem,* and many base belief in unverifiable ancient writings. Assertions are said to be of vital significance in living correctly, but these assertions are mere fiats stemming from Holy Books of dubious provenance, which lack confirmation.

So, the first question might be on what grounds should we believe that any immaterial spirit exists, immaterial consciousness or immaterial world of spirit in existence.

That such can be imagined is obvious. People also believe that immaterial existence as imagined is possible. But why?

There was some time ago, now rather less fashionable, of a Spiritualist cult. It was, still is if extant, highly derivative on common Christian and other religious beliefs. Seances reportedly communed with spirits of deceased people, old buildings were reported to be haunted and devotees claimed evidence of "ghoulies and ghosties, and things that go bump in the night." The meme lives on, less confident, and rather downcast.

While enthusiasts continue to seek contact with those who left the conversation, actual evidence is immaterial. No reason to believe has yet materialised. Large popular support for Christianity and kindred religions has supplied a population which is well acquainted the notions of metaphysical dualism. The language and conceptual support were ready for these guesses at immaterial existence, but no good reason to believe was forthcoming. The meme has replicated, but the reality of an immaterial spirit world is unproven. The spirit world, you might say, lacks substance.

What is presented as reason to believe metaphysical dualism is persistence of that speculation in the religious writings of some major religions. That people fear mortality, prefer living, and mourn the loss of those who die is eminently understandable. The antiquity of religious belief in life after death is not proof of veracity, it only establishes the widespread influence of the early search for answers to speculation about beginnings, no doubt from times when man first made God in his own image.

It is amongst the various creation myths, inventive tales from before even the possibility of astronomy was conjectured, that such mythic accounts of beginnings belong. Example, the book of Genesis begins with a dualist account in which God exists in lonely splendour before calling earth into existence by an act of will and then creating fish, birds, animals, and finally Adam with Eve for company. Man was given, at the beginning, dominion over all the earth with its creatures. Eve was then relegated to obedient status after yielding to the serpent's smooth talking and eating fruit forbidden by God. A bit rash for her to be so insubordinate in the circumstances.

Now, *there* are some memes that replicated: man's dominion over the earth and its creatures and another, that woman cause humanity's fall into sin. Yet another, that woman is subject to man. We need not here pursue the outcomes of the popularity of those memes, or the difficulties created by humanity's exercise of dominion[27].

The book of Genesis has been a fertile propagator of many memes contributing to religious and other folk beliefs. One wonders whether we would ever had heard of Judaism, the Gospels, or Christianity had Genesis not captured early expressions of these memes.

---

[27] Dennett, "The first rule of memes, as it is for genes, is that replication is not necessarily for the good of anything; replicators flourish that are good at ... replicating!" p.203

We cannot know. But as Dennett points out, meme replication is not devoted to the good of anything save memes themselves. The memes which together convey the religions of the world, so prolific, spreading so contagiously have produced many folk beliefs that are mistakenly thought to be knowledge, contradictions overlooked.

This contagion has had millennia to gain hold of people's imagination, to gain the appearance of authority both by popularity and by their antiquity. It has spawned the various religious myths and been responsible for well-established institutions and writings now deemed to be Holy and commanding.

These samples show well-known examples, but all memes, not only those of religious matters, replicate. Sometimes to our benefit, sometimes not at all to our benefit. Biblical advice to avoid building a house on sand is wiser that some other.

My plea is to exercise caution and prudent discretion when claiming knowledge, by ensuring that the claim is on sound grounds, and refusing to accept mythology or the advice of sages and traditions of folk beliefs as grounds sufficient to bear the weight of established truth.

"Sounds good; believe it" is a meme readily replicated.

Readily reproduced, but not good for anything but error.

PERCEPTION AND REALITY

During the process of evolving, the progenitors of our species developed central nervous systems of enough complexity for self-consciousness to emerge. What possibilities were then evident for cognition and language, or awareness of the self-consciousness of conspecifics, are not recorded.

However, an ancient puzzle about self-consciousness has generated much subsequent philosophical speculation. Our perception of others, observation of their actions and vocalisations, remains *our* perception. The perceptions had by other people, their mental states, are not perceived directly by us – we observe their reactions, hear their response, even hear them describe what they are seeing. But the only insight into their awareness and thought is what they choose to reveal, plus our assumptions based on what we perceive. All sensory impressions are private: one may describe them, or say what one thinks has been sensed, but one's hearers cannot *experience* one's sensations.

An individual moving, interacting, sensing can easily assume that "seeing is believing," that they are directly sensing an external world as it is. This is our normal experience. We may later wonder about the external world and other people.

Then one might realise that although other humans speak of their experiences and perceptions, those experiences and perceptions are not part of our own sensory experience (save as assumptions formed during perceptions of other people). We do not share their experiences or perceptions.

So, we become aware that our perceptions of the world about us are also *ours* that the perceptions of the world for other humans are thus *theirs* in the same private way. Observing other, non-human beings in their variety responding to their environments might well engender curiosity about how they perceive the world such different perceptual equipment.

It is easy to assume that true beliefs about the world are conveyed by perception, especially since experience of responding to perception is effective, and the environment is perceived as relatively stable. But "best available theory" replaces direct contact with reality when it is recognised that multiple-eyed spider perception must be unlike human binocular vision, and both are unlike the sonic perception of bats, and all vary from canine perception by sense of smell – yet all successfully negotiate the same physical environment.

Our evolution with increasing complexity of our central nervous systems leaves structured responses. Priority is given to survival, safety, and sustenance – we are an evolving animal species. Then comes any other business at hand. The growth of social bonds, of ethnic identities and centuries of history lead to complicated demands on our thought and action

The privacy of perception leads to each individual to believe that they perceive the world directly. Humans became aware early of this privacy of perception and in whatever form a question arose as to how one person's perception of surroundings differed (as often it does) from their own. Some philosophers have woven theories from this, exploring knowledge, dismissing metaphysics.

So, is knowledge of the world and of other people possible?

Not in the sense of knowledge that is certain, secure, and permanent. All attempts to construct a theory of knowledge necessarily depend on assumptions – there is no source of authentic or guaranteed truth – prehumans had to find ways to grow social communities, to develop communication, to stay warm and to defend themselves. Modern humans still make assumptions that lead to learning about societies, about science, and about people. Some major assumptions underlie our theories of knowledge. Can we assume Berkeley's position, that only minds and perceptions exist, or should we take a realist a realist stance?

Is an individual more than a consciousness of sensations? Even awareness of one's own body, of physicality, is sensed. In the 18th century, George Berkeley said that "to be is to be perceived" and held a view that only minds and mental activity exist. The notorious question "If a tree falls in the forest and no one is there to hear it, does it fall?" reflects Berkeley's opinion that material substance does not exist, that objects are collected ideas or sensations existing in minds only while they are in mind[28].

While conceding the privacy of sensation, others oppose such idealism as Berkeley's and favour a realist view of objects, the world and other people[29].

Samuel Johnson's attempt to dismiss Berkeley in summary fashion by kicking a stone on the road while exclaiming "Thus, Sir, I refute Berkeley" was fruitless. The pain in Johnson's toe, the scuffed boot tip, the cloud of dust, and the sound of stone slithering over pavement, not to mention the appearance of audience and surroundings would all be dismissed in phenomenalistic[30] description by a follower of Berkeley.

A realist could agree with this attribution of sensations, yet believe that there was a material stone, and boot, and that Johnson's was a physical action, and reject the idealistic account of the incident

---

[28] Berkeley, Third Dialogue, *Berkeley Philosophical Writings, p.179.*
[29] It is germane to recall that the notion that no material thing can think has played a part in related debates. It lurks behind Descartes' *"cogito ergo sum"* and his laboured explanations of animal activity.
[30] Phenomenalism was described by Warnock as "Berkeley without God" at p.236.

Prominent early awareness of disparity between perception and an external world is Plato's analogy, the imagined cave in the *Republic* suggesting that we humans can be thought of as captives bound deep in a cave, facing a rear wall which is lit by light from cave mouth to show shadows of figures near the light - which is all that the prisoners can see. Those shadows are the only contact the captives have with reality. The *real world* is unknown, the shadows which captives see they accept as reality, but they are mistaken - reality is the unseen, represented only by shadows.

One ambition of many thinkers has been the acquiring of absolute knowledge. Few make that point so explicitly as Descartes:

> Not indeed that I imitated the sceptics, who only doubt for the sake of doubting, and pretend to be always uncertain; on the contrary, my design was only to provide myself with good ground for assurance, and to reject the quicksand and mud in order to find the rock or clay.[31]

Aspirations to absolute and certain human knowledge faced the challenge posed by the private nature and obvious differences between individuals led to conclusions like Berkeley's. So, certainty was sought elsewhere. Both Rationalist and Empiricist philosophers spent much effort and ink seeking to achieve it.

A major attempt to deal with individual perception was to seek knowledge certainty in the rationalist use of *a priori*[32] argument, the validity of which was not based on perception. Medieval proofs that God exists are well remembered samples but fail as proof. Such argument relies on an already known (or believed) premise, something innately or axiomatically true. John Locke's arguments against innate knowledge advanced early empiricism, and *a priori* bases for knowledge are scarce[33].

---

[31] Descartes, Discourse on the Method, Part III.
[32] Prior to experience, innate. Metaphysical argument often employs it.

Hume argued that we could consider our beliefs about the world but could not base knowledge on sensory experience.

Kant, aware of Newton's empiricism, writes of a noumenal – phenomenal distinction, also based on the unknowability of noumena, "things in themselves," which cannot be known save by inference from perceptions[32].

Empiricism, depending on sense perception also finds certainty elusive: the individual restriction implied by the privacy of perception, and the errors known to attend perception showed that human knowledge so attained lacked the certainty then thought characteristic of real knowledge. The search for absolute certain truth, was admirable but mistaken.

Humans, at least many in historic Europe, had believed that they were unique, a species specially created by God as uniquely conscious and thoughtful: some even believed that they were responsible caretakers of God's creation. An argument is possible that advances in human thinking and knowledge were retarded for some centuries by adherence to such convictions.

Charles Darwin and others freed them from such delusions[34]. The human species evolved, developed consciousness and language. Finally

---

[33] Locke *Essay Concerning Human Understanding,* 1690. He criticised Descartes, was friendly with Isaac Newton and Robert Boyle and aware of the science of the time. [32] *Pure Reason* means *a priori* reasoning. Further, Kant believed that "our inner experience is possible only on the assumption of outer experience", assuming that there is an outer world. Also opposed to metaphysics by the Vienna Circle and English Logical Positivists, Bertrand Russell discuss "sense data".

[34] To the grave offence of conservative Christians, Darwin found humans to be a species of evolving animal. We have learnt a lot, we have made mistakes, we can rejoice about much, but we are limited. Knowing everything is a fantasy.

learning much about the world they developed communities. Late in that process they learnt that their learning was fallible, often needing correction. Along with their myths and folk beliefs a strand of knowledge about the earth and each other took shape, new experiences, trials that failed – or succeeded – reinforced what they thought or showed the need to think again.

Perception matters. Locke got that right. But it is not the whole story. We now think twice before asserting that the mind is a *tabula rasa*[35] at birth. More time passed, and perception received some help, instruments, electronic devices, scientific research, mensuration critical analysis all sharpened or corrected perception. Perception arrives through many external and artificial channels.

Realising that absolute, certain knowledge is not at command, and that fallibility is universal to humans is a starting point for seeking knowledge, as it is for considering what we mean by the truth of our knowledge. Assumptions are dictated by the fallibility of private individual perception. Fallible does not imply *always wrong* but it does mean *able to be mistaken*. If our perception is wrong, and we suspect or learn so, we normally try again perhaps using other senses.

It is rational to assume that the world is consistent with what we perceive, assume that our perception of the world (although our own) is as accurate as possible for one with our sensory equipment. Included in that perception are other human beings and we take that perception to be real. Berkeley's response is to deny the existence of all bur the sensations

Fallibility is the essential notion underlying claims to truth of claimed knowledge. When an idea or experiment is not a success we are prompted to think again. Success enables appropriate interaction with

---

[35] A blank slate.

the surrounding reality and with other perceivers. Intersubjective agreement on perceptions confirms

Berkeley responds to the privacy of perception by denying material reality, seeing all as individual perception. But that demands his heroic theory to accommodate apparent shared experience. To assume that the world and its inhabitants are existing entities as they appear, is less audacious than the immense and complex an act of creation Berkeley attributed to the individual's mental states as if *they* constituted the world's existence and the multitudinous acts and opinions of those characters the individual perceived or learnt about.

A realist view of the world and of people is a rational basis for a theory of knowledge. It still makes a fallible assumption, inferences from individual perceptions. An assumption gained, not by guesswork, or extra-terrestrial magic or traditional folk beliefs, but by problem solving, and testing possible answers.

SPECULATION AND PIETY

Knowledge and Mythology above argued that guesswork, tradition, mythology, and religious beliefs *do not count* as knowledge. People do hold such beliefs: But this is just a mistake. Books revered by the faithful of any religion express the beliefs, the commitments, of believers – which is not a proof of those confident beliefs. Undoubtedly people *think* such beliefs are true: but thinking them true is *just a mistake.*

There is a profusion of such beliefs and other competing belief systems – there are some thousands of Christian sects. Because of the time and place of this writing its argument largely concerns Christianity[36].

Any belief, however asserted by people with sincere intent and based on traditional teachings, amounts to no more than speculative chatter if not supported by knowledge established with sound evidence. Piety does not guaranteed truth. I do not doubt that the beliefs held by many Christians known to me are sincere: but think due diligence about beliefs has been lacking. No doubt this lack is to be understood in the context of Christianity's long history and its role in the culture dominating the now decrepit British Empire. Many theological educators and scholars are vulnerable to a too-convenient reception of views conforming to orthodox accounts of tradition while ignoring the paucity of evidential historical support for those views. Many of the

---

[36] Other religions face similar issues, but I have no need to pursue them. Not that religions other than Christianity are to be favoured: the duality involved in others fails for them, as it does for Christianity. Arguments (like those of "near death" experiences) unashamedly imply dualistic beliefs as if they were evidence. The argument here is quite generally a rejection of beliefs that humans have access to, or are receivers of, nonhuman (divine or "other worldly") information sources.

faithful lack familiarity with the issues, and the powerful historical cultural influences are usually no incentive to notice them.

Permit me to expand on reasons for making this assertion.

But the Bible says ...

Of central importance to Christian believers, are sixty-six books (some add the books of the Apocrypha also) collected and called the Bible. Usually Biblical readings are prominent in services of worship, sermons are Biblically based, and much scholarship is engaged in exposition and analysis of the collection often referred to as "The Word of God." Christian Theology is usually Bible informed, and doctrines judged by consistency with it. As "The Word of God" the Bible is thought true; for fundamentalists infallibly: others hold more liberal opinions.

Twin myths pervade the Biblical writings, since these myths are characteristic of ancient Hebrew thought, and were central to ancient Hebrew religious beliefs. These myths are implicit in the Biblical literature (as in most ancient writing and Holy Books). No wonder they persist popularly still despite lacking evidence of truth. Testing the truth of such speculated beliefs from various Holy Books is not possible.

These legends of religious belief are influential in much thinking about life, death, and Divine judgement. One is known as metaphysical dualism and takes two forms in popular thinking. First is belief in an eternal immaterial world of God, angels, demons, departed souls, contrasted with the temporary material world of humans. Another popular form of this myth holds that a human is an eternal soul to be judged by God and which has a perishable physical body.

This ancient belief is founded on fear of mortality and inability to imagine a world not designed by a personal creator[37].

One can readily see the attraction for a legendary after-life. Such a belief allows suitable quarters for immaterial deities and their attendants. Indeed also, that an account of good and evil (transcending mere human naughtiness) is presented as a cosmic battle between sources of right and wrong, a Righteous Deity and a Prince of Darkness. This account is varied by different religions. The dramatic richness of such mythologies holds great interest. But the only evidence we have for these are the differing Holy Books of religions. Easy to appreciate also is this expression of a hope that life's inequalities and immoralities will find final justice done even if post-mortem. The human desire for such beliefs is evident, though divine wisdom is less apparent.

Another supporting myth is that physical events in this material world are affected by forces, spirits, deities, demons, acting by non-material means by miracles, magic if you like. The Bible holds many miracles, many attributed to Jesus, as well as a resurrection and redemption achieved by blood sacrifice acceptable to God. These days talk of miracles usually of situations unexpected or not well understood.

Holy Books are no more than accounts given by ancient religious believers concerning their own beliefs and practices. They are human writings. Tales of myth and magic are unremarkable in ancient religious writings. The Bible is not divine oracle, superhuman wisdom or command, but simply records written by fallible pious humans. Later in the first three centuries of the Christian Era, to collected Jewish scriptures were added selected Christian writings, gathered well after the time ascribed to Jesus by the Gospels. This collection is now Christianity's Bible, venerated at worship, studied assiduously, and often called "the Word of God" by the faithful though nowhere so naming itself – the final collection occurred long after the original writers were deceased, none having been aware of the later collection of

---

[37] Who seems equipped with superior wisdom and knowledge but as Feuerbach insightfully recognised appears modelled on *homo sapiens*

their work. The contents of the Bible reflect the judgement of churchmen over a century later, who assembled the Bible. Cooler heads are advised to read this collection as an anthology collecting human accounts of ancient religious belief, as intimate glimpses of ancient beliefs, but not as words from heavenly realms.

Viewing the Bible as Divine instructions, as infallible truths including advance information about apocalyptic end times is an implausible misunderstanding of its origins and authority. Because endorsed by tradition and powerful emphasis by Church worthies and frequent reinforced in liturgy and instruction, the superstitious reverence accorded Scripture is powerful. But mistaken. It is refreshing to read the Bible with new eyes: it can change perspectives, even after years of conditioning.

History is not as favourable to Christian tradition as is often assumed.

Considering this issue is often evaded, but the earliest years of Christianity and the developments of churches, is not as well-known as many of the faithful might wish. Bold claims relating to ecclesiastical history are grateful for traditions which seem more like Chinese whispers. Kenneth Scott Latourette, a Christian historian of fundamentalist bent[38], no wild radical certainly and not famous for rocking boats, has observed that

> The complete story of the spread of Christianity in its first five centuries cannot be told, for we do not possess sufficient data to write it. Especially is our information for the early part of the period provokingly fragmentary [38].

---

[38] Once a Baptist Missionary in China, historian, prolific author and Professor at Yale Divinity School. His multi-volume work, *A History of the Expansion of Christianity* (1945) was my companion through Theological Studies. [38] *A History of Christianity* p.65.

An earlier generation spent considerable effort and ingenuity in searching for "the historical Jesus" without great success. Enthusiasm was dampened by a lack of evidence to support Gospel accounts. Set in a period when the Roman Empire flourished, and Palestine was under Roman control there is an absence of mention of Jesus, any claim to be King of the Jews or of his Crucifixion in Roman records. Indeed, there is a lack of reference to the life of Jesus in any literature other than the New Testament writings[39]. The few times the name of Jesus appears in non-Biblical literature are only thought of as evidence of Jesus' historicity when a sizeable dollop of wishful thinking assists those who yet hope for historical certainty. This emphasises that evidence about a historical Jesus is rare, some say non-existent other than the New Testament documents. This lack of support from other historical sources consequently leads some writers to suspect Gospel records as promotional efforts by a new sect. Ancient religious records are boosted by accounts of supernatural doings which tend to strain credulity. I need neither to develop the point, nor to endorse it. A debate whether there was an historical Jesus occurs, suggesting that the Jesus of early Christian tradition was perhaps an invention of one of the mystery religions[40]. It is not germane to this article, although the question might give pause in the context[41].

I take it that there is no call to pursue another fairly common argument sometimes advanced in defence of religious commitment. This

---

[39] I recognise that various other legends exist (example, that "England's green and pleasant pastures" were visited by Jesus) but do not feel a need to deal with them.

[40] See Freke, T. & Gandy, P. 2003. *The Jesus Mystery: Was the Original Jesus a Pagan God*. Element. Hammersmith. Other references include Aslan, Reza. 2013. *The Life and Times of Jesus of Nazareth*. Allen and Unwin, Sydney. Carrier, Richard. 2014 *On the Historicity of Jesus. Why We Might have Reason for Doubt*, Phoenix, Sheffield.

[41] Those quoted were all born after Gospel accounts of Crucifixion: Josephus (c.37CE), Seutonius (c. 69 CE) and Tacitus (c.56CE). All wrote well after the dates usually accepted for the life of Jesus. All mention Jesus, none claim eye-witness status, and their sources are unclear. Hearsay about a recent development in Hebrew religion? Or?

approximates "My life is as predicted by my faith: I believe as my faith directs, and my inner experiences confirm it." Or "my experience is evidence enough." Perhaps it is sufficient to indicate that adherents of any religion are well conditioned in the emotional experiences to be expected by those believers who are faithful to their creed. And avid evangelicals seem unlikely to be enthused by visions of the Blessed Virgin, Catholics at Mass rarely break into choruses of gospel harmony while devout Buddhists feel no surge of emotion at mention of the Kabbala.

To think more clearly about beliefs about Christian origins, the New Testament books, the Gospels, it helps to remember that whatever claims are made about Divine establishment of the Church(es) and Scriptures, they are human institutions. However else it is described, a Bible is unmistakably a human physical object said to be written by human beings, historically produced, translated, edited, and studied. Churches are human associations arranged and governed by political processes, often hierarchical. They are housed in substantial buildings known historically to dominate towns, and financially supported to some extent of considerable property and wealth, including art and other collections. They exercise much influence on public and political decisions, and not infrequently have their beliefs on moral questions enacted in laws that non-believers must obey. So, no matter what claims are made about special status as ordained representatives of Deity, the churches are human institutions, governed fallibly by humans, able to act because sustained by human resources and making decisions (whatever liturgy and prayer they employ) by entirely human processes of argument and voting. And changing their minds. Miracles take a little longer!

They are human institutions like any other having consequences for other humans, for societies, and personal welfare of individuals. Some of these consequences, I am more than happy to record, are beneficial. There have been times when churches have (however imperfectly) championed moral cases[42]. Churches have supported educational efforts (less worthy when aimed at proselytising) and charitable assistance for the needy, on occasion they have supported civil and human rights, have even attempted to influence politicians against unworthy policies. It is only just to acknowledge consequences of a positive kind. There is also, not surprisingly, a record of negative consequences due to these human institutions, however they claim origin and authority attributable to God. But I do not need to list these, some of which have been in public discussion for a while. You do not need a list from me: and will probably be glad enough without it. Dark coloured pictures are not needed. But more need not be detailed. These effects range from individual mental illnesses, attitudes to sexual and gender questions, relationships, constraints on personal choices, influence on political decisions, even reaching to foreign policy which ignores serious problems of poverty, disease and peace. Times have even seen use of military force to spread a faith, or significantly exacerbate warfare. The point is, that there is no good reason to think that your religious beliefs – influenced by your location, your ethnicity, and friends – have disclosed truths of immaterial realities or superhuman dramas as conceived in ancient Jewish folk lore. There are just so many colourful religions as alternatives, claiming for their Deities recognition as the one true God. Human imagination is powerful, human aspirations for immortality often urgent, and human access to fictional superhuman existence and power so impossible. Ambition overreached often fails! You and I can be content with human status and the constraints of human life. We have so much actually to celebrate. Life offers so much in real challenge, so many possibilities, our loved ones, our children's discovery of life and learning, so many ways to be. Imagination even hope and joy. No need

---

[42] Although claims to moral authority, or to encompass the source of morality, are overblown. Commandments and moral recommendations are routinely accompanied by promises of reward or threats of punishment (heaven and hell are prominent), so much that is presented as moral advice is actually in control by appeal to self-interest.

to fancy eternal life. No matter that what we imagine living infinitely might hold. Imagine if it were boring! Hopefully not a Sunday School picnic. Enough is enough.

Our resources, like our world, abilities, time, and energy are finite.

FAITH'S VIRTUAL REALITY

I subtitled an earlier book *Faith's Seductive Virtual Reality*[43].

Let us explore that notion. We think of our everyday world and its people as reality. Faith envisages another reality: an immaterial, spiritual dwelling of God, attended by various angels, caters for the *post mortem* souls of humans, and is rebelled against by Satan and demons.

This is believed to be eternal by contrast with the everyday world which will vanish in an apocalyptic denouement in God's control. It is not merely a view that heat death will finally overcome the sun.

Reality, in the everyday world, holds choices for people, lifelong. Organisations, businesses, families, friends, the business of living and loving, disagreeing and conflict caring for pets, thinking about conservation, worrying about climate change... The lot. It keeps people occupied.

Then, maybe because God is thought to be critical of idleness, the faithful have put considerable effort into emphasising this spiritual world and finding in it the focus for life's purposes and activities, We are advised to "take no thought for tomorrow," to "make peace with God" and to devote life to such faith, obedience and service that we will *post mortem* inherit the kingdom of Heaven. The locus of life and responsibility is this speculated spiritual realm, and what we mistakenly take for reality is just an extended trial which determines our real fate as either eternal bliss or endless punishment (exclusion at least).

So many devote their lives to this virtual reality, and frame their earthly life to conform with the teachings of their chosen religious sect. Some security is called for before making so serious an investment.

---

[43] *Abandon the Cave*, 2012.

Be curious. What assurance would you require to commit your life, devotion, and service to this *virtual* reality? Incentives are clear enough. To begin, clear forgiveness of sin, a good conscience supported by the God on whom all care can be cast. Guidance and direction are also offered. Fears of mortality are assuaged by hope of resurrection, eternal life, and Heaven as life in God's presence. Not to mention an escape from what are reputed to be the unquenchable flames of Divine punishment[44],

What might give one pause, despite such blandishments, is that when one considers the matter, these incentives are promised by some groups who believe that the seductive virtual world is a true account of reality, and guarantee the promised bliss. The whole notion is a religious belief, not universal: the Islamic afterlife for instance, rewards quite different behaviours with apparently sensual rewards. These religious beliefs commonly lack sound evidence.

The evidence for the seductive virtual reality of the Christian message is that it is the teaching of various ecclesiastical bodies, not known for factual rigour where dogma collides with knowledge gained by human rigour in investigation. Known, rather, for decisions resting on conclaves of believers who, despite claiming Divine guidance, have made declarations after decisions reached by garden variety human argument and voting procedures by clerics not averse to toeing orthodox lines.

The human decisions of churchmen (preponderantly men) are claimed to rest on Divine truths, derived from "the Word of God." But that claim itself is no better than teachings resting on Scripture. The Bible gains its authority as God's Word, not from any actual evidence, but because the faithful have declared so, and liturgy constant repeats that ascription of authority when speaking of the Bible. The Bible,

---

[44] Metaphor or not, it is grim to contemplate.

despite its reputation as messaging from God, is an anthology of ancient religious writing in which believers express their religious beliefs and practices at that time. It is not infallible. It is not divine. No extra-terrestrial intelligence dictated its content. It was itself collected long after any of its contributors, even the latest of them, were long dead (none knowing anything of this collection). Those who decided what was to be included, what discarded, amongst the available literature was a group of churchmen[45] whose divine guidance and reliance on sound evidence was no better than that of church councils whose decision in retrospect are all too human.

Custom and tradition play a role in forming and focussing various institutions. The role is important. But these are not sound bases for claims regarding the truth of opinions and beliefs.

It is possible to invest one's belief and life's effort in vain pursuit of so seductive a virtual reality.

---

[45] Council of Nicea, 325 CE. The Vulgate Bible was translated as a volume in Latin in the late 4th century CE.

SHE'LL BE RIGHT, MATE!

A popular colloquial Australian saying. It is often praised, or boasted, that characteristic of a characteristic "Aussie" attitude is relaxed confidence or being "laid back" in a time of stress or difficulty.

That attitude reflects a calmer and more accepting approach when problems present, than does anxious care or panic. It may stem from optimism, perhaps from courage or determination. Acknowledging difficulty or that what one faces is problematic, it may express commitment to dealing with what is in hand or solving the problem. Over-anxious and flustered response in those situations tends to make for less efficient responses and less well considered problem solving. At times problems are feared because of anxiety or uncertainty, and an assurance that all is well might lie in the common call.

But a ready call that "she'll be right, mate" is inappropriate if it rests on bad information, mistaken belief, or guesswork. A confidence not supported by ability or an awareness of how to go about solving the problem is mere bravado, when an unsolved problem or difficult situation calls for more substantial response than wishful thinking or hollow assurance of easy success. The expression is vacuous also if it means no more than someone unnamed will "fix it."

Situations have arisen during the coronavirus pandemic in which those who have taken an attitude that "she'll be right, mate" have found confidence misplaced. Sad outcomes have mocked beliefs that is amusing to attend Covid-19 parties, when individuals who have done so become infected. Others have learnt to their great distress that their belief is false that God protects believers from disease. There have been many for whom social distancing, and avoidance of close crowd contact have been deemed to be bureaucratic interference, have been enlightened as the gamble that they were unlikely to be infected was lost. Then too there are those, usually in the USA, who are so confused about freedom that they consider their individual rights to ensure freedom of decision and assembly are so powerful that they override government restrictions limiting inter-personal contact (on public health grounds during a pandemic crisis). A Darwinian solution springs to mind, but I suppose that is unkind.

In those instances, "she'll be right!" is sadly wrong.

AUSTRALIA'S RACISM

America is convulsed with demonstrators chanting accompanied by civil unrest as I write in mid-2020. The same agitation, with less rioting, is in Australia also, crowds mingling Indigenous and white-skinned people have gathered under the slogan **BLACK LIVES MATTER.**

High time!

America's grim history of slavery has been slow to see African Americans, most descended from the six to seven million slaves imported in the eighteenth century. The Civil War was fought over slavery, and other issues, but segregation continued. A Civil Rights Act was proposed in 1964, and finally passed in 1968. African Americans had previously served in the military and navy during several wars, early and frequently as orderlies or stewards. But generally, race discrimination was oppressive, and inferiority assumed. A disproportionate police severity pursued African Americans and the unnecessary death of one man following his death[46], under the deliberate pressure of a police knee choking him has inflamed mass protests. The country erupted with the Black Lives Matter cry. The glowing embers of the still festering aftermath of the Civil War were evident in the divided community and Administration responses.

1968 was so recent. The underlying hostilities have their home in racism.

But then, Australia, for all its claim for the notion of "a fair go," is just as racist as Trump territory. On 10 August 1967 following a referendum in May[47], the Constitution was amended to include

---

[46] This year.
[47] 90.77% voted yes.

Indigenous Australians in the number of Australians. Citizenship had still to be negotiated for some. Aboriginal people were no longer classified as "fauna" as in the previous Federal Flora and Fauna Act.

Britain had been involved in the slave trading of the eighteenth century, but abolition of that trade was well advanced when Australia was settled. The new colony escaped the importation of slaves that has had such consequences for the United States. But Australia's founding as a colony of Britain was as a penal settlement, a place of punishment to which people troublesome to the powerful in Britain could be sent, remote from England.

The new Colony did not recognise Aboriginal existence. Seen as savages, their culture was dismissed and their aeons of living in this land unrecognised. They were not seen as another nation with whom negotiation and diplomacy were required, but lawless savage natives to be dispossessed and replaced. Cajoled, on occasion, but repressed if difficult. Later as the colony in New South Wales became one of several, then federated to become the Commonwealth of Australia, racism in the new British outpost affected attitudes to any ethnic group other than English derived[48]. Chinese in goldfield days, immigrants from Europe (even from England) were aliens to be kept distant, and the twentieth century wars in Asia brought others to these shores, whose ethnicity troubled "true Aussies." Many from other parts of the world initially were dubbed by some (usually pejorative) colloquial name (Kraut, Dago, Pommy, Slope). Time moderated strangeness. By degrees grudging acceptance taught Australians some benefits of other cultures, cuisines, and music. Multiculturalism crept into the national consciousness, which however still clings to racist attitudes. Some groups still advocate "white supremacy."

The sad and deplorable reality is still, so long after British invasion of this continent, and despite (grudging as it has been) the

---

[48] Even in mid-20th century English migrants were marginalised "Poms."

developing multiculturalism, Indigenous Australians have been kept on the edges of society. They have not been welcomed as true Australians despite their
occupation of the land thousands of years before others invaded it. The tribal and clan structures of centuries have been ignored, languages not just forgotten but outlawed, customs wantonly suppressed, and families separated. As noted above, for two hundred years Indigenous Australians were not recognised at law as human beings, Australian citizens[49].

I have written on this theme previously[50] after listening to Stan Grant speak at a Newcastle Writers' Festival, and reading his book *Talking to My Country*. Watching on television his reactions to brutal treatment of imprisoned Indigenous boys in Donsdale and finally his Four Corners report concerning the Black Lives Matter disturbances, more than ever I believe Australia must come to terms with its past, must begin to be honest about the racism behind the massacres, and other attempts to make the problem of displaced original inhabitants go away[51]. With few exceptions, black Australians have been accepting and patiently advocating, for full acceptance into this society. Their response to the barbarity of historic treatment at the hands of white settlers and government has been restrained. White responses have sometimes been crass and inhumane, as evident in the earlier "white Australia" policy and the attempt by some prominent Australians to dismiss any question of past abuses as a "black armband" view of history. The country has been foolishly insensitive in avoiding a patent need for some truth and reconciliation process.

---

[49] Despite this, all the wars have seen Aboriginal men serve the military.
[50] Racism's Long Shadow, in *Leave Heaven to Angels and Sparrows,* 2020 [51] Professor Lyndal Ryan continues to map massacres of Indigenous Australians in history. (University of Newcastle, NSW)

It is well past the time when this country needed to confront the issue of race relations, when it must accept Indigenous people without patronising condescension, as citizens and not as a minority to be corralled.

A telling tale. A stepson rented accommodation in a group of Housing Commission flats which saw some petty crime and occasional local disturbances. Some locals were known to keep weapons including knives and handguns. The complex held a considerable number of people,
including some drug users. A group of Aboriginal families lived there, near his residence. This group were to be heard making racist remarks about other (white) residents and threatening some, including the newly arrived stepson. This was some time ago when he was a young adult. Reasonably, he found the Indigenous group quite threatening as their open conversation indicated. I tell the story because it amplifies discussion of racism. He kept to himself and avoided provocation.

Undoubtedly, he had views unsympathetic to the ethnically significant Indigenous group. Racism is endemic amongst Australians.

Whatever influences his attitudes had on his views of his neighbours was matched by their "reverse" racism. One can understand an Indigenous racist reaction to the predominant white lack of acceptance or understanding of Aboriginal culture and values. It is still an "us versus them" issue. In a way that epitomises the wider problem. Many Indigenous people have expressed a desire to be understood and accepted, and wished that Australia might resolve its past and the divide between descendants of the original inhabitants and the population stemming from those who have arrived since Arthur Phillip arrived.

Paul Keating in his Redfern speech of 2014 reminded us emphatically that it was the new white arrivals who had separated Indigenous people from their lands, and introduced addictive substances, and that leave Aboriginal people in the socially outcast status and dispossessed position that feeds much of the negative opinion that is common enough amongst white Australians. Victim blaming is not high ground we should wish to occupy. The attitudes and actions of many Australians has been condescending and patronising, sometimes contemptuous and excluding. The "white Australia" policy saw deliberate attempts at government level to see the Indigenous people disappear, while children taken from Aboriginal families were raised as white.

The history of racism is world-wide and long. Ingrained attitudes such as these are not quickly re-thought or forsaken. But racism and its divisive effects pose problems that humans should work to resolve.

We cannot here see the whole picture of historic racism, and the thinking that feeds it. But it has a history, for instance, there was a Hamitic myth in pseudo-ethnography, now discredited, that an invasion by European black Caucasians invaded Africa. Another form has it that Noah's son Ham was the distant ancestor of the black Africans. A Bible anecdote tells that Ham saw Noah naked and drunken. In rage Noah cursed Ham's son Canaan to the effect that his offspring would be "servants of servants." The story was thought a justification of slavery by some[51].

Regardless of skin colour, or facial appearance, every human is a member of *homo sapiens*. For all our differences of language and culture, whatever our history, and however our politics differ, we owe it to each other that our relationships are not driven by mindless prejudice, or easy prejudged ascriptions of the attitudes and beliefs of other people. We must not assume that one from a different ethnicity must display characteristics we observed in their fellows. We will surely differ. But we must be aware of cultural and educational differences, variations in

---

[51] No need to spend time now, but a Google search is informative.

social mores and pressures. At the least, we cannot ascribe the present situation to Indigenous nature: they have been separated from land and traditions, treated badly, introduced to addictive substances. White Australians have contributed a racist response to this land's original inhabitants. We need skills in negotiation, in acceptance, or at least understanding, and the grace to allow difference in others.

In particular, it is our task to complete Australia's unfinished business in respect to truth and reconciliation about our history and the original inhabitants of the continent, and to reach genuine reconciliation in citizenship and in personal relationship terms.

DEMOCRACY

Various nations are prone to boast their systems of governance as superior. Often repeated is a claim that "democracy might have its failings, but it is the best form of government available."

But the term "democracy" is vague: used variously merely because citizens vote. There are comments to consider. What concerns me quite is the nature of our boasted democracy. The people elect representative at all levels of government, in theory.

Actuality our "two party" system ensures that the people do not alone decide who is to be nominated and elected. It is true that independent candidates may self-nominate and if sufficiently supported, may gain election. But the two major parties have extensive organisations, access to funds, and employ advertisers and organisers. Each electorate faces a preselection ballot to choose a local candidate at upcoming election. In some cases, strategic considerations are cited by State or Federal councils of the major parties to *impose* a candidate for an electorate. This is popularly called "parachuting" a candidate into an electorate without involving a vote by local members. So, effectively in this event (not usual, but frequent enough) even the local members are denied a vote. The Candidate for election is imposed by party machinery[52].

Democracy in ancient Athens lies behind the modern notion. Athens, a local city not an extended nation, when making choices allowed at most several thousand men to vote. At that early time, only citizens, free men, were eligible to vote. Women and children,

---

[52] I reveal that having been a member of the Australian Labour Party I resigned when my local branch (without a vote) was assigned a candidate by State Council.

as well as slaves and noncitizens were not voters. Decisions about current events rather than election of representatives called for a vote which was usually by raised hands. Ostracism, exile of those seen as troublesome, was by casting pottery sherds. So, the fundamental notion lay in a vote of *some* citizens (as above, restricted), a vote of the people.

Ancient Athens was aware that free male citizens were not all equipped to vote on important civil matters at mass meetings. Not all were literate, not all were aware of issues, not all were well informed. Even is this city-sized polity it was evident that many citizens might have little to contribute to the city's decision making. Plato famously wrote of three classes of men. Philosopher kings, promising children educated from childhood, rigorously trained and experienced in city affairs, until in older years they could rule. Guardians, a spirited military class, soldiers so trained, and finally an acquisitive group (οί πολλοί – "hoi polloi" the many) workers, the masses of people not widely educated. This indicates that from its early days, democracy was aware that not all participate in communal decision making with equal interest and information. Plato's stratification of the population is not adopted in modern democracies, which assert that voting is by the people, and resist notions of a ruling class with incapable underlings. Similar differences amongst voting communities are not adopted by modern democracies.

Australia is proud to name itself a democratic nation. Its electoral system is believed to be free from manifest corruption, elections are orderly and held as due. There is a not uncommon belief that the nation's relatively small population elects far too many politicians. Three tiers of government: local councils, State parliaments and Federal Government of the Commonwealth of Australia. Personally, I favour enlarging the regions and electing

Regional governments and a National government. Federating the states following the British annexation of the country may have seemed a good idea at the time but now the simpler and leaner arrangement would seem preferable. That matter is not about to be resolved: although traditions grow quickly, their root systems are emotionally resistant to change.

In systems like ours, it is accepted that some voters consider personal advantage, or irrelevant matters, in casting less well considered votes. Politicians appeal for voting victories, and attempt to attract the largest number of voters, and in Australia many eligible to vote are less well educated, or indifferent. One obvious problem is that politicians importantly appeal to acquisitiveness – "what's in it for me?", and "will I pay less tax?". Often this is when costly public works or other schemes which might well be in the national interest or improve the nation's manufacturing or export capability are more obviously needed. Informal ballots are lodged, compulsory voting satisfied, and indifferent citizens escape a fine, or the disinterested cast no vote. Perhaps our careless approach to leaving education to be divided between the States and private (often religious) schools results in a lack of awareness of civic responsibilities and pertinent social issues.

Political parties attract donations and powerful and wealthy groups donate, clearly pursuing their own interests. These interests, those of the fossil fuel companies and miners generally, and of the larger commercial concerns for example, attempt to cultivate agreeable relationships with government. Lobbyists have a busy time.

Contemporary Australian understanding is that adult citizens of both genders (with a few legal restrictions) exercise a democratic vote in the election of representatives to councils and parliaments, and rarely enough, at referenda on selected issues[53]. But this view of universal adult suffrage is not the whole story, since the organisational power of the two major parties has led to an electoral system which promotes antagonistic confrontation on party issues, affecting political debate and electoral opinions. Policies are frequently framed to advance the interests of politicians and political parties or lobbyists, immediate matters of national interest or individual welfare may wait.

Presumably, democracy would benefit from an adequately educated and informed voting population. An added benefit would be political parties which governed in the national interest rather than in narrow terms of personal abuse aimed at winning power by whatever populist promises. An earlier essay draws a sharp distinction between knowledge based on integrity of scholarship and research, and beliefs founded on the uncertain grounds of folk beliefs, mythology and religion. Unfortunately, education in Australia is divided between public and private schools. The latter are frequently maintained by various religious organisations, not a few fundamentalist or traditional Catholic, other Churches, Jewish or Islamic·

The Saturday Paper records that between 2009 and 2018 "total funding for Catholic and independent schools, in real terms, grew more than five times that of public schools.[54] " I believe that religious instruction is a concern which should be in-house for each religion. The school curriculum should be a national one and should be uncensored in relation to subjects involving ethics, science (biology[55] in particular) and history. That is, education in this

---

[53] It must be admitted that enrolling long dead citizens or pet animals sometimes boosts parties concerned.

[54] July 11-17, 2020, p.6., An economist advocate of Save Our Schools says that in the same period in Western Australia public school funding was cut by $1417 "per kid" and Catholic and independent schools had increases of $1170 and 1749 respectively, per child.

secular nation should at base be secular[57] and should advance personal development characterised by intellectual integrity. Time currently wasted in public schools allows militantly proselytising groups as well as well-meaning but often ill-educated scripture teachers to inculcate their own forms of belief amongst often indifferent children. That time would be more usefully spent in classes on humanistic ethics, civics, or personal development. Or on an understanding of the social politics of Australia.

Although political parties, and electoral committees, even candidates might struggle with the notion, it would be a great advance in Australian democracy if electoral advertising, and the policies advocated by political parties, addressed an educated public concerned with national interest, the welfare of the disadvantaged and dispossessed, with education and health. We have far too much political appeal to individual hip-pockets, and concern with economic interests of the already wealthy. The politics of fear exacerbate threats of terror or possible foreign motives and appeals about law and order are not always justified by statistical evidence. An appropriate funding by federal government of political parties, possibly proportional to share latest electoral voting, is advisable. As is control of donations to minimise pressure from interest groups (commercial or union) and to avoid what seems an American custom, undue influence from wealthy supporters.

I do not need to elaborate further. Regrettably, politics in Australia has reached a low point. Political infighting within and between parties and party factions is commonplace, a determined Christian Right threatens to control the conservative parties, the old

---

[55] Religious beliefs have no credibility in negations of science. The fault line, again. [57] Religion is free, religious peoples' beliefs are not to be suppressed and religious instruction should be an activity of religious bodies as much as worship and observance of religious festivals and holy days. But not the role of education in schools.

Country party (now the Nationals) more actively promotes the interests of the mining (or fossil fuel) lobby than those of the farming community while the Labor Party ineptly loses sight of its historic concerns in order to find a middle ground acceptable to voters. Ideological voting for major parties at elections is losing ground as voters as trust in politicians fades. Political leadership plots seem more concerned about personal achievement and disciple gathering than about policies. We could use some real statesmen and women.

SECULAR STATE

Australia is a secular state and must remain so.

With no established religion, no established Church, this secular society is proudly multicultural, while its population has a diminishing majority of adherents to Christianity. Individuals and groups remain free to practise their various religions, but not to interfere in matters of government, legislation or administration

Although Australia was founded as a secular state, determined efforts over time have led to regrettable compromises. Churches and Church schools are exempt from taxation, some Church organisations are counted as charities. Religiously affiliated politicians have gained some ground in legislation on matters deemed moral by Churches like marriage and gender issues[56]. And politicians heed the views of leaders of major Churches, given the number of voters involved. If Parliament were to support policies and principles which compromise the nation's secular nature, whether by enacting legislation or providing financial support, it would be alien to the nation's Constitution.

Any Prime Minister of Australia is entitled to hold religious beliefs and to practise them, as is any citizen. I take no issue with our Prime Minister's religious beliefs, whatever the religion[57]. Mention of religious issues has been notable in the press, and aspects of this issue occasion this essay which expresses no opposition to religious freedom other than insisting that Australia remain a secular state. This essay holds no wish to limit religious freedom of belief and worship but does oppose attempts to impose

---

[56] The late Senator Harradine is well remembered.
[57] In an increasingly multicultural society, it cannot be assumed that a politician is Christian. For the record, I was once a Christian clergyman but am now atheist.

beliefs and value judgements of whatever religion through law or administration.

It seems that our current Australian Prime Minister Scott Morrison, avid for popular approval, embraces the odd Shire-like persona ScoMo[58]. *The Monthly* has drawn attention to the Prime Minister's unfulfilled talk "about what's in here" (indicating his heart) and discusses "what we know about the prime minister's Pentecostalism". His Pentecostalist belief is much proclaimed though neither articulated nor clarified. This essay was initiated since lack of clarity in what was offered as frank revelation leaves speculation and uncertainty whether these religious beliefs might unduly influence legislative matters or administrative arrangements.

Unlike most other Christian groups in Australia, Pentecostal groups (variously named, these days) and some fundamentalist believers interpret some scriptural passages as foretelling an apocalyptic end of the world. This interpretation has been repeated frequently over the previous two thousand years, yet unfulfilled. Attempts at announcing an impending apocalypse have been many and mistaken[59]. Biblical passages have been believed to refer to the circumstances of each age by those expecting a prompt divine judgement: imaginative interpretation is involved. It is a farfetched suggestion that scriptural writers two millennia ago had the United States, Russia, and China in mind (or some such). Prime Ministers have not usually envisioned the end of times to be near. Perhaps now we need to consider why personal beliefs not widely held by citizens, are not good bases for national decisions. We do not become a republic even if a Prime Minister believes we should, nor do we declare war whenever he is convinced of another nation's ill intent.

---

[58] "Scotty from marketing" is preferred by one newspaper.
[59] See R.B.Y Scott, *The Relevance of the Prophets.*

Pentecostalism is loosely defined on belief issues, less articulated by creedal conformity, but is more noted for its emotional responses. Which Pentecostalist group claims one's allegiance gives some indication of whic h beliefs are in question.

If ScoMo's beliefs are as *The Monthly* outlines them and he shares his sect's apocalyptic vision it is important to know if government policy is affected a view rare amongst Australians. Indubitably, Mr Morrison asserts sincere adherence to beliefs including, it has been alleged, both that he holds office because God wants him to rule Australia, and that God guides his daily actions and decisions[60]. Does this influence his approach to issues of policy? Does belief in an imminent apocalyptic justify ignoring climate change or choosing Jerusalem as the site of our embassy in Israel? It is just such religious convictions which could risk influencing government policy, and which call for vigilance to insist on the nation's secular status.

The nation's present state and its readiness for the future must be framed by actual present data, not by sectarian interpretations of ancient religious writings.

Emphatically, if his beliefs regarding Jerusalem or climate change are formed by religious convictions, one raises no objection *to his beliefs*. But secretiveness about them, and lack of reasons of state based on data, gives rise to uncertainty. Transparency denied is inimical to democracy, especially at times when public trust in

---

[60] Any conviction that the PM is divinely guided each day is emphatically also not shared by those many other Australians who are Islamic, Hindu, Zoroastrian, Buddhist, Shinto (you can fill out others known to you), not to mention other Christian believers, from whom Pentecostalists are keen to be distinguished. Recent census figures suggest (would you imagine?) that a significant number of Australians are atheist and believe government policy should be framed by sound research, not in Donald Trump's style.

politicians is uncertain. Failure to speak the relevant whole truth, or withholding significant information can give rise to scepticism. Playing poker with the electorate, holding tricks unrevealed to the electorate, is less than admirable.

Emphatically, I have no desire to limit the Prime Minister's religious beliefs. Religious beliefs are many and varied. Some might consider that those beliefs are mere human attempts to invent comfortable answers to existential questions or perhaps just another version of Christianity.

But if those beliefs, being sectarian views neither shared by the population generally nor supported by relevant public service research, contribute to forming government policies, they become an exercise in religious domination which would have left the late Senator Harradine envious.

Our Prime Minister relies on his conviction that the Bible, the ancient religious writings important to most Christian groups is an actual divine revelation of the supernatural and the future. Most Christian believers do not share the apocalyptic faith that "end-times" are imminent, an unfulfilled belief that has held total disappointment for numerous sects throughout the past two millennia. The odd claim of literal inerrancy involved in fundamentalist thinking, and belief in "tomorrow's news today," is rejected by most. Believers in other faiths do not share somewhat erratic certainties about the apocalypse.

One does not doubt that the Prime Minister's religious beliefs are sincerely held. If those beliefs inform his political thinking and priorities, as one must assume since he is proud to proclaim so, the electorate might well wonder whether his non-disclosure of beliefs of an imminent apocalypse in any way relate to his "captain's choice" regarding Jerusalem. One trusts that policy decisions are based on better evidence than sectarian beliefs dismissing climate change issues as irrelevant, or religiously formed views that Jerusalem figures in an apocalyptic denouement.

The absolute right to hold religious beliefs does not confer any mandate to impose on our country decisions based on sectarian religious beliefs.

Incidentally, the PM has no right to assume that his sectarian beliefs *will be fulfilled*. A measure of modesty might determine that religious views can be mistaken, that views on biblical interpretation might be fanciful, or that prophesying the future is an enterprise with a history of shamanistic failure.

The electorate is entitled to government guided by researched data, not by partisan religious clairvoyance. It requires genuine transparency and a government for today's multicultural nation which eschews devious religious manipulation.

RUDOLFPLATZ 1976

In Germany on study leave, I rented a flat in Köln[61] from one Frau Weiler. It was a flat which had obviously been furnished as accommodation on floor four of a commercial building, but the bathing facilities were a telephone box-like structure in the area which served as kitchen and living room. One grew accustomed to this but christened it "the tardus." At the time my son Ian accompanied me, and he soon made friends with a group of students. This had the advantage that I heard colloquial German spoken as well as formal high German of the University.

For a good time in the German winter, late in the year, my daughters also came and stayed with us in Rudolfplatz and we enjoyed time together. The girls also had fun in the snow and exploring this city's great museums and art, and its 2000-year history. Jane and Stephanie, twins, turned 18 while there, so we took a train to Paris for a celebratory dinner. Christine who has her degree in fine art spent time in galleries amongst paintings and sculpture. I have an array of photographs of the Kölner Karneval, the crowd-choked city and the elaborate floats and costumes of the parade.

My middle adolescence saw the Second World War, and I was prepared at school to fight the enemies which included Nazi Germany. Training as an army cadet I was prepared with actual weapons, ammunition, and rifle range experience in exercises which on occasion included aircraft overhead firing at a point ahead of us. So, it was salutary to live and study with German people, experiencing normal courtesy and behaviours, learning that war's

---

[61] City on the River Rhein on territory historically occupied at times by France or Germany, now West Germany.

depiction of foes tends to see only brutal people acting atrociously. True, some people do act badly, but meeting normality is a corrective relief to such negative war-time vilification.

Mid-year vacation took advantage of a Eurail pass, with trips to London, Paris, Madrid, Rome and Vienna, even Berchestgaden. Brief
interest-filled visits fuelled unfilled travel ambitions. But we saw some great art, visited the birth houses of Mozart and Beethoven, and soaked up the ambience of places which history books mentioned but now were living experiences for us.

We lived in a pleasant location overlooking a public area of the city which then called Rudolfplatz, had been known earlier as Adolf Hitler Platz. In 1975 the Platz held a pleasant small park and we looked from front window directly at the massive gate tower, the Hahnentor, remainder of the medieval wall to the city.

Köln was earlier a Roman colony[62], hence the name, and it is still possible to find traces of the Roman city boundaries. Later a larger medieval city grew, enlarging the settled area and ringing the old colony. At several places remain traces of the medieval wall, and beyond it a typically modern sprawl. The magnificent Kölner Dom, the cathedral by the river, is adjacent to a museum displaying Roman relics. Early in my time there I began to explore the cathedral. As I walked into the nave I was quite overcome by the atmosphere of this ancient place. Light streamed from high clerestory windows though the softer and rather dimmer space and I was amidst such history and tradition that emotion bid me escape to the open air. A memorably moving moment. I had quite a few years before forsaken religious belief, now my reaction on entering that space was not religious but rather a sense of awe. The architecture, the antiquity, the ambience and especially the illumination stirred

---

[62] Colonia Agrippinensis now Köln, later Cologne when France ruled.

me. I again visited the cathedral later and often, listened to its organ, and explored its memorabilia.

One special occasion was when a good friend, the artist John Martin who was working in Basle at the time came to Köln to visit me, bringing a couple of bottles of good Hunter red to celebrate my birthday. Next morning, we visited the cathedral, which was crowded for celebration of a festival honouring the Three Wise (or Holy) Men. The Kölner Dom treasures a large golden sarcophagus as that of the three visitors to the birth of Jesus. The densely packed congregation was listening to impassioned sermon, and I was trying to translate so that John was aware of what we saw happening. The sermon became quite agitated and vehement as the preacher for the occasion made it plain that his hearers must vote for a named party. On hearing this, John (very much of a different political persuasion) marched off. He did wait patiently in the square for me to join him. I had stayed to enjoy the organ display.

I had chosen the University of Köln because I was teaching a course in Kant's philosophy at the time and took the opportunity to learn more in discussions other than those I had heard at home. I also attended classes in German language since I needed first-hand experience of the language spoken without translation. Talk about immersion! No supporting English explanation, one spoke and heard only German, and could be presented with a local newspaper to make sense of headlines and everyday reporting.

The Kant seminars were a revelation. They were formal. The empty-handed Professor led a small procession into the lecture theatre. Following was the professor's assistant, bearing the great man's books, and a small group the function of which I did not learn. Participation was a useful experience. My skills in German were enhanced also. The years have passed, and I regret to record that my need to maintain that language has been no more than occasional, and now requires an exercise of memory when an extended or unfamiliar German work is examined. I recall with mixed chagrin and amusement that in a crowd watching the Kölner Karneval, a couple behind me from out of town overheard me talking, and remarked "Er spricht als ein Wuppertaler" (He speaks like a country bumpkin).

We spent almost full year in Köln. As the year passed and winter closed in, the cold became dominant, the skies often overcast and the nights longer, I grew eager for home and sunshine. My memories linger, and I remain grateful, not only for the way study was made available, and the immersion in a different language and culture, but also for seeing the old world, being a stranger in an alien city, and that the experience could be shared with my son and my daughters.

PHILOSOPHY

What is called philosophy is too often no love of wisdom and no studious pursuit. Philosophy is frequently needlessly mystified by those wanting to peddle some esoteric creed or addled cult. Some attempt to attract credibility to their cause by representing it as "love of wisdom," philosophy. Cartoons show unkempt gurus in hilltop caves reached by exhausted climbers seeking some secret of life or path to bliss.

That is not philosophy as I know it.

I taught Philosophy in the University of Newcastle from 1967 to 1997 though certainly not seeing myself as a guru, or as particularly wise: certainly not the guardian of esoteric secrets to living, success or happiness. My studies in philosophy began when I realised a need to clarify my thinking about beliefs and looked for skills in logic and critical thinking. It was refreshing to learn and argue various writings from different perspectives. Especially stimulating was seeing ethics as a rational decision-making process and arguing reasons for endorsing beliefs. Only later came the time when these studies had finally concerned work attempting to justify description of God depending on analogies, that I was engaged to teach in a Department of Philosophy.

Often, I would begin an introductory session by displaying ambiguous pictures. One classic can be seen initially either as a sketch of on aged crone, or as a comely young woman, another as a comparison of two cars (one of which, in a second picture, is shown as a toy model seen in perspective, distant from a full-sized vehicle). Then discussion followed concerning the possibility of error in perception, mirages, mistaken identity of well-known friends, and such.

Conversation would range over the vagaries of perception, consequently of belief, and differences experienced by students about various issues. Then we would begin to search for understandings about why we were all in a group to study philosophy.

As time passed lectures increasingly engaged students in argument about issues. At times I played "devil's advocate" to engage students in discussion of questions: I looked for reasoned argument rather than rote memory regurgitation of lecture material.

Regrettably, philosophy is presented and understood by students (all too often by their instructors too) as if it were a History of Ideas, introducing ancient and modern philosophers and their systems. This is a valuable enough exercise, educational in broadening thinking and developing the capacity for considering differences of view. Logical and critical thinking is usually enhanced in a course on philosophy.

There is a sense, however, in which philosophy is closer than is often realised to its ancient Greek sense[63].

When we survive what must be the startling experience of being born, the world is alien to us, and we have no idea of how we might live or behave. Initially we find ourselves unknowi8ng about our world, and slowly are moulded by parents and environment. Our learning is then moulded by ethnicity, gender, language, class and wealth, religion, education, parenting and the circumstances of place and time. The confusion of beliefs and opinions, the pressures from others, and relationships. Wars, famines, good times and bad all stir the pot of difference.

---

[63] φϊλοσοφία 1. love of knowledge and wisdom, fondness for studious pursuits 2. the systematic treatment of a subject, scientific investigation 3. philosophy (Liddell and Scott Greek-English Lexicon, abridged)

Philosophy returns to such questions as "what sort of world is this?" and "how should I live in it? as starting points.

So far from esoteric, guru-like pronouncements, philosophy works at basic questions each person needs to confront, regardless of this confusion of conditions and time. We may well profit from some of the writings of our predecessors. We may well be thankful for disciplines which long since were separated off from philosophical wonderings. But philosophers still have those basic questions impelling their efforts. They are not vague speculators about esoteric mysticism. They need the knowledge of our world, and of people to fuel, sometimes to shape, their studies. They also have a watching brief over methodologies and a duty to critically analyse reasoning. In Philosophy of Science, or of History, for example, their role remains significant.

My own university in Newcastle, New South Wales has followed some others in accepting government and commercial pressures, by emphasising its role of preparing students for employment, undoubtedly part of their brief. The cost has been at the expense of humanities studies in recent times, partly because of misguided government policies. The Philosophy Department of previous days no longer exists: a few philosophers remain to teach courses of ancillary disciplines. There are academics in other fields who hold mistaken views of philosophy as if it wasted time on vague speculation and wordy argumentation about issues of no practical purpose. Just as there is wisdom in the slogan "don't believe everything that you think," it is well to consider the effects of what our knowledge enables, whether what we build, or the technological development so promising in immediate view is ultimately detrimental.

The University of Newcastle has flourished, does many things well, in engineering, medicine, biology and research – not least in education of Indigenous Australians (especially in Medicine) and in supporting entry to tertiary studies by adults who previously were denied that opportunity and younger people who were disadvantaged.

There is a case for reform in Australia's university system. I believe that we have now a disproportionate number of universities for our limited population. Some rationalisation, perhaps by uniting some institutions, perhaps by specialising some disciplines at fewer universities would help.

The universities are often wealthy institutions and need to change their hiring practices: too many academics are casually employed, and not always paid appropriately. At the same time, some Vice-Chancellors and higher echelons of administrative staff are paid excessively, and staff for administration rather than research and teaching is too strongly emphasised.

We have not the same access to wealthy endowment as many American universities. The distances in our continent justify strong regional universities. Perhaps existing vested interests might make the process difficult, but reform is necessary.

POSTSCRIPT

I trust that your reading has been rewarding, and that you have had, as it were, a conversation with me. You have been generous enough to consider my opinion on several matters. Whether we have reached agreement, or some points of contention is for you to determine.

It is by now obvious to you that religious beliefs have supplied a theme for several essays. That is no accident. I was in youth a devout and active evangelical Christian, after teacher training and three years in country schools I left for training, four years in a theological college. That time saw me thinking about faith, growing a familiarity with Biblical matters, and developing skills appropriate for pastoral ministry, my goal at that time. The study ended my dalliance with fundamentalist views of Scripture, despite the single minded and industrious attempts of my teachers at the time. I served briefly as pastor of a Baptist Church. No longer at home with attitudes, and unconvinced about aspects of belief, I resigned and petitioned the Presbyterian Church to accept my services. There followed further training in the Theological Hall at St Andrews College in the University of Sydney. These were the days before Church union in Australia. Set study fort two years there, I was given further reading but completed after one, as the Professor of Theology there was satisfied with reading set for me, and I went on to serve as Parish Minister for the following eight years.

By that time, I had grown much more independent, had found Parish work rewarding and the wealth of experiences and interaction with people in so many life situations a sobering and maturing way of life. I had also been rethinking my beliefs. The time came when I did not really think it honest to continue. I was more concerned about my doubting of beliefs, such as about life after death, less comfortable with devotional exercises and aware that I was increasingly becoming more humanistic in sermons and practical advice. I was no longer an orthodox believer, and my beliefs were in some disarray. I resigned the Parish, which by then was the historic St Andrews' Church in Parramatta, once the scene of John Dunmore Lang's work.

I briefly worked as a casual teacher in Public Schools. I was then father of three young children, and without employment had little financial support. Soon after my time in the Theological Hall I had completed an Arts degree with honours in Philosophy and was working toward my PhD. I was working at gaining skills and better ability to deal with beliefs. Good fortune came, the Professor of Philosophy in Newcastle University had offered me a position in the Philosophy Department, which I felt unable to accept because of my recent taking the Parramatta Parish appointment. When I was no longer employed, he offered me a tutorship which I was glad to accept and developed my academic career. I worked in that University until retirement.

This tedious personal history supplies some background to my thinking, and to my present attitude.

There are other essays, too. A couple concerned democracy and the importance of Australia's remaining a secular state. Others reminisce about foreign travel, living in the present, being certain, virtual reality, delusion, racism in Australia, and some issues facing the teaching of Philosophy.

Some essays have circled around reasons for belief and are influenced by the difficulties attending my own development from early fundamentalist piety into intense commitment and finally through increasing uncertainty to doubt and then rejection of once treasured faith. Now happily atheist, I am content with that history.

I think it worth revealing thus, because too often discussions of religious belief are lost in antagonistic argument and unthinking hostility and mutual rejection. I hope it is clear, that while arguing as the atheist I am, I do not think that others *must* agree with me, or that those who retain religious faith are somehow less worthy[64]. Those who insist on terminating discussion with anyone holding views different from their own lose the opportunities inherent in wide human difference and valuable thinking inherent in other people's insights.

Friends who were fellow students while training in a Baptist college have maintained comfortable lifelong contact, despite religious differences. My respect and regard for many who were my parishioners so long ago has not been diminished by my changes in belief. I agree that much value is gained in the fellowship of shared beliefs and gathering, in music and architecture (though some modern structures lack charm), cooperative efforts in charity, and in mutual support and encouragement. Churches function as human institutions and succeed in meeting many human needs. That I believe that evidence is against religious faith does not mean that I have an aggressive or belittling attitude to believers[65].

As human institutions churches also commit human failures, sometimes grievous. At times they are less than kind, seek to control other lives and impose their moral beliefs on all the faithful and

---

[64] I retain good friendships and deeply respect, many from this past. It would be dishonest if I did not add that I have known some whom I believed to be hypocritical, others who sought aggrandisement (either in control or in wealth): and that aggressive proselytization is arrogant as well as mistaken.

[65] As with any other human institution, I am aware that good attitudes and actions of the godly are frequently accompanied by mistakes and moral failures. Good, bad, and moral I calculate in humanist terms, not in respect of divine commands.

other religious groups, and the population generally. Arrogance and domination have blighted Church history at times. The reader does not need a catalogue from me: the daily press is sufficient.

I have not written to offend, and with no belief that missionaries for Atheism are needed. It would be passing strange if one ancient religion were privy to truth without question, and more than odd if intelligent creatures were created by a God but denied questioning curiosity.

It alarms me that powerful beliefs can dominate the thinking and living of so many people, when those beliefs are accepted without real care about their truth: authoritative words from tradition or gurus or even from significantly wise lips fall short of sufficient proof. So, my writing is aimed at stimulating consideration of some of the issues that arise.

You who read what I have to say about those issues owe me nothing, certainly not reluctant agreement. I do not believe that eternity depends on religious decisions or rejection of religion. I think that the concept of eternity, of eternal life, is overstimulated fear of mortality. You are, as far as I am concerned, free absolutely to dismiss my writing. Life is yours to make it what you will, and I rejoice in your freedom and hope that you flourish.

YOUR REFLECTION

This is an aide to reflection on this book's treatment of a fault line in popular thinking.

It is easy to claim truth, we are all too well aware. It has been known to be shorthand for "I want you to believe ..."

The following page is FOR YOUR EYES ONLY.

The author does not want to know your thoughts about it.

It is personal and private; no reader is invited to plumb any other reader's reactions.

THIS IS **NOT** A TEST, NO ONE NEEDS YOUR RESPONSE.

DO THE WORDS BELOW DESCRIBE YOUR RATIONALE FOR HOLDING IMPORTANT BELIEFS?

HONESTY,

PROBITY,

INTEGRITY,

RECTITUDE,

RIGHTEOUSNESS,

PRINCIPLES,

IDEALS,

MODESTY,

VIRTUE.

FOR YOUR PRIVATE USE

NOT FOR QUIZZING OTHERS.

ABOUT THE AUTHOR

 Ralph Robinson PhD who retired after a career that began as a schoolteacher, spent 15 years in Theological training and practising as a parish clergyman. Since 1976 he taught philosophy in the University of Newcastle NSW and finally directed the university's enabling programmes for four years. Interests are education, theology, philosophical discussions of belief (including logic, epistemology, theory of mind as neuroscience is advancing).

Because too often discussions of religious belief are lost in antagonistic argument and unthinking hostility and mutual rejection. I hope it is clear, that while arguing as the atheist I am, I do not think that others *must* agree with me, or that those who retain religious faith are somehow less worthy

Youthful sports were swimming and tennis; he later crewed on a yacht racing on Lake Macquarie and once to Hobart. Busy with teaching during the early years of the then new University he served in the University Council and Academic Senate, and other administration. Since retirement he has kept himself actively thinking, writing, and hopefully out of mischief. He thinks that important beliefs do not usually depend on folk beliefs.

Content with life, happily married to Shirley Schulz-Robinson, his son Ian Ralph, daughters Eleanor Jane, Stephanie Ruth Kaul and Christine Kay, five grandchildren and a great grandson. He is grateful for Eleanor Jane's skills in cover design, and to friends who have been supportive.

A slow learner, in his later years, he has learnt to be content.

BIBLIOGRAPHY

Aslan, Reza, 2013, *Zealot: The Life and Times of Jesus of Nazareth*, Allen & Unwin, Sydney.

Berkeley, George, *Philosophical Writings*, ed. T.E. Jessop, 1952, Nelson Philosophical Texts, Edinburgh.

Blackburn, Simon, 1999, *Think*, Oxford University Press, Oxford.

Carrier, Richard, 2014, *On the Historicity of Jesus: Why We Might Have Reason for Doubt*, Phoenix Press, Sheffield.

Cornford, F.M. 1941, *The Republic of Plato: Translated with Introduction and Notes*, Oxford University Press, Oxford.

Darwin, Charles, 1859, *The Origin of Species, 2011 edn.*, Collins Classic, Hammersmith.

Dawkins, Richard, 1989, *The Selfish Gene*, new edition, Oxford, Oxford University Press.

Dennett, Daniel C. 1991, *Consciousness Explained*, Penguin, New York

Descartes, Rene, 1637, A *Discourse on Method, Trans John Veitch*, 1957, Dent, London.

Feuerbach, Ludwig, 1841, *The Essence of Christianity*, trans. George Eliot, 1947, Harper, New York.

Freke, T. & Gandy, P, 2002, *The Jesus Mysteries: Was the Original Jesus a Pagan God?* Element, Hammersmith.

Grayling, A.C. 2007, *Against All Gods*, Oberon, London.

Latourette, Kenneth Scott, 1954, *A History of Christianity*, Eyre & Spottiswood, London.

Liddell and Scott, 1953, *Greek-English Lexicon*, abridged edn. Clarendon Press, Oxford.

Locke, John, 1690, *An Essay Concerning Human Understanding*, 2 vols., 1959, Dover, New York.

Mearsheimer, John, 2011, *Why Leaders Lie: The Truth about Lying in International Politics*, Duckworth Overlook, London.

Plato see Cornford.

Robinson, R.M. 2012, *Abandon the Cave: Faith's Seductive Virtual Reality,* Strategic Book Publishing and Rights Co., Houston. *Leave Heaven to Angels and Sparrows,* 2020.
Scott, *R.B.Y.* 1944, *The Relevance of the Prophets.* Macmillan, New York.

INDEX

Made in the USA
Columbia, SC
11 October 2020